T0299558

Emma Lamb

The Loop Journal

A New Path to Self-Discovery

Welcome to Loop:
a choose your own path journal

To begin your journey immediately, turn to page 8.

What is Loop?

Reflection is an essential part of understanding ourselves and making meaningful change in our lives, but it's not always easy to do. In fact, it is really hard to understand the process behind what we think or do or feel. Much of our behaviour feels instinctive and the pressure of everyday life often means we don't have time for reflection. Is it any wonder that we keep repeating errors? Even when we try to learn from our experiences, we often return to old patterns.

What would a better option look like? First, imagine having the insight to see the impact of upbringing, learned routines and personality on your thoughts and actions. Then, imagine having the courage to consider alternative ways of being and, finally, the daring to follow through on your plans. This is the purpose and premise of Loop. Its primary goal is to give you the tools and space you need to reflect on who you really are; to consider the range of voices and experiences that have led to the creation of this self, and to dig deep to find the image that is most representative of you now. This process of self-exploration is the goal itself. This isn't a journal designed to make you do anything. You don't have to exercise more, or say yes less. But you do have to examine why you do or don't do those things – and whether you really want to do them anyway. Loop will help you filter through the noise.

Loop's origins

I am a coach, trainer and teacher, and I keep seeing talented people who feel like failures, promising individuals who are stagnating, and intelligent thinkers who get stuck in repetitive cycles. Modern life is challenging: too many deadlines, too many competing voices, too many tasks and no time to consider what we really want. On the other hand, I witness the tremendous capacity for change and development on a daily basis. The difference between these two scenarios is the ability to reflect, and the best way to build reflection into your life is by journaling.

Although many argue for a daily journal practice, the strain of modern life might make that impossible. I don't want you to aim for something, and then not achieve it and give up on Loop. Instead, be realistic and kind to yourself. What time can you guarantee yourself in a week? Two to three sessions of ten to fifteen minutes each week is about right. It means that when you sit down you will be really focussed, and that you have time to reflect between each session.

Journaling with Loop

Loop is rooted in my experiences and supported by research. If you want to know more about the ideas behind Loop before you start, you can go to page 156, although I recommend waiting until you've done at least a few exercises first. Here are a few notes to get you started:

Loop is a totally different approach to journaling. Rather than boxing you into a predetermined or chronological route, the format puts you in control. At the end of each page you will usually have a choice of two or three pages to go to. You can go in whichever direction you choose.

Loop has a realistic rhythm to it. Each page of the journal is designed to be completed in ten to fifteen minutes. Do it in the morning, in a coffee shop, on the train or after dinner.

Sometimes Loop will send you back to a prompt you have already completed. These are opportunities for 'Double Loop Learning' (see page 156), although they are not the only ones.

As you use Loop, go easy on yourself. If you are finding it hard to concentrate, give journaling a break that day. Do it when you are feeling in the mood and are prepared to be honest. You might also find that sometimes you don't want to complete an activity. That's fine – you can skip it. But first ask yourself why you don't want to do it – is it a style preference? Is it avoidance? Sometimes doing something that wouldn't be our preference makes us think in a different way and can shake up rigid thought processes. Don't give up too easily. The old adage of 'fake it till you make it' has stuck around for a reason. I often find a slow start to a session can be worth pushing through. It is just your brain settling into the process. Sometimes you just need time.

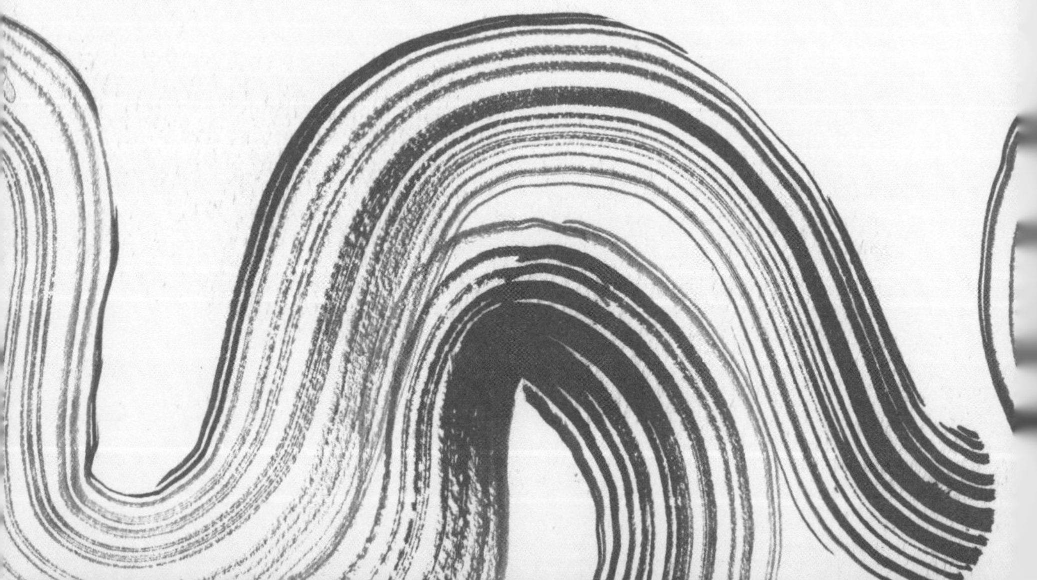

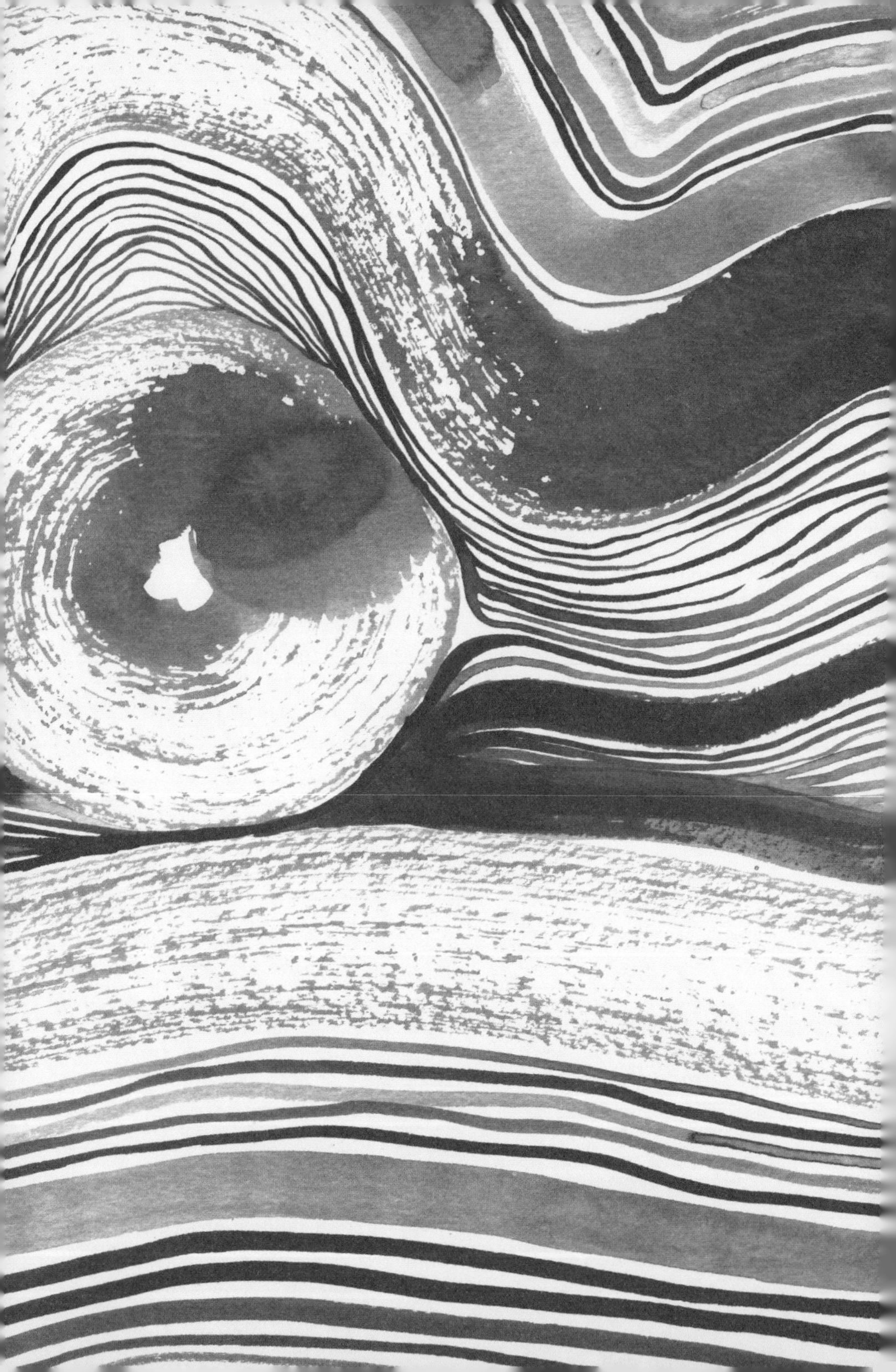

It's in your hands

Whatever the issue you want to examine, you will benefit from challenging questions and time to think. I know from my work that there is a real need for this type of help, but it has to be active and self-directed. Change can only happen if you want it to and Loop is designed to put you in control.

Ultimately, Loop can't actually do anything without your willingness to try new things and engage with the process. It is built on useful techniques and full of helpful activities, but they will only be impactful if you want them to be. Loop is a tool not a plan, and a process not a goal. You have to choose your own path and create your own solutions.

What Loop *can* help with is discovering who you are, what you want and how to make it happen. Working with Loop two or three times a week will refine your skills of self-awareness and increase your self-efficacy. You will develop an awareness of the power of your own voice. But there is no intended outcome of the journal other than the one you set it.

The beauty of Loop is that you can pick up right where you left off. Don't worry about how it looks, or about always using the same pen. Do it when you can and when it fits. Remember, the tasks are not dated and are driven by your mood and needs. The journey is self-guided: you can't succeed or fail. It's just about you, as you are, as you are meant to be right now.

So, be kind to yourself. Be brave and honest. **This is an exciting journey and it begins on** **page 8.**

It's time to take stock

The beauty of Loop is that it assumes no particular start point.
Wherever you are on your path, Loop will walk alongside you.
Take this moment to capture the beginning.

What is happening in your life at the moment?

How do you see Loop as being helpful to you?

What are your motivations for starting this journal?

What ways of thinking and being do you wish to have more of?

Your Next Choice

Consider your wishes on page 66, or go to page 112 to assess the power of words

Yes, you can!

What do you need to give yourself permission to do?
Will you?

Your Next Choice

Get nostalgic on page 117, or tune into yourself on page 106

Backwards bucket list

Instead of thinking of all the things you are yet to do, celebrate the things you have. Write a bucket list in reverse. What have you already achieved and experienced?

Your Next Choice

Look back on page 93, or get positive on page 137

Hope

What makes you feel hopeful?

How have your hopes changed as you have grown up?

How has hope affected your decisions?

How can you protect hope?

Your Next Choice

Examine patterns on page 24, or reflect on relationships on page 76

Flow

What activities make you lose track of time and other commitments?
How does it feel to be in flow? How can you experience it more?

Your Next Choice

Find out what matters on page 77, or go to page 127 to start changing

Missing pieces

What do you see in other people's relationships with friends, family or romantic partners that you feel is missing in your own? How important is this to you? What steps could you take to change things?

Your Next Choice
See it from both sides on page 134

Interest map

1. Use these spaces to gather all the things that interest you. How do these things connect?

2. What is your passion?

3. Where, if anywhere, do these interests seem to be out of sync?
Which areas of the map would you like to give more attention to?
To what extent does work reflect your interests?

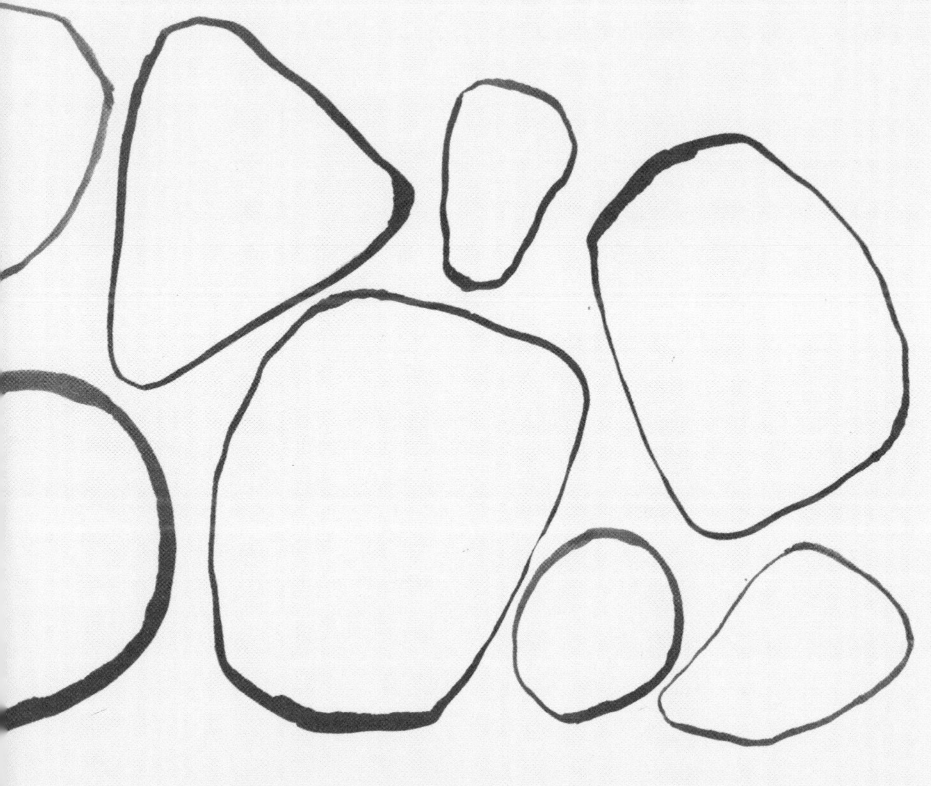

Your Next Choice

See change happen on page 127, or walk with pride on page 73

Guidance

Throughout your life there will have been mentors – official and unofficial – who have guided you. Focus on the people you have been inspired by. What did they do? How did they inspire you? How did they demonstrate confidence?

Your Next Choice

Loop back to page 105 and consider what satisfaction means to you

Perfect

Perfect is impossible. How do these words feel to you? **Good, satisfying, excellent, enough, fantastic, secure.** How would it feel to have your work or cooking or life described as them? How would things change if **'good enough'** became the new perfect?

Your Next Choice

Loop back to page 145 to reassess your feedback, or find some flow on page 79

Positivity

Fill your cup with positivity, ideally make it spill over.
Collect all your happiness and magic here.

Your Next Choice

Consider your fears on page 142, or loop back and look at life differently on page 25

I am not

Who are you not? What are you not?

Is that good/bad/indifferent? Why?

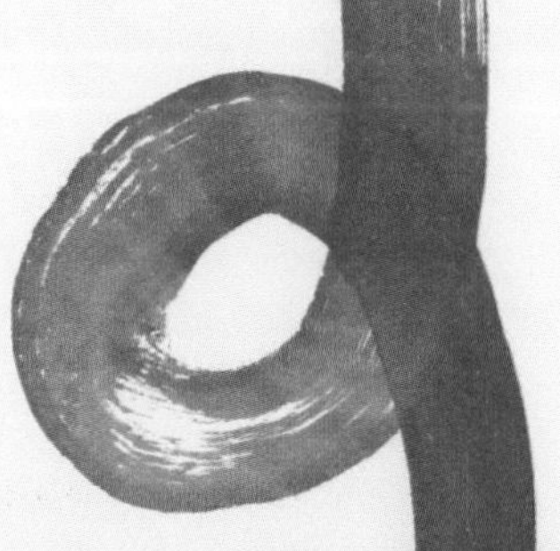

Your Next Choice

Loop back to something bigger on page 65

Family values

In my family, when:

things go wrong we...

someone is ill we...

people talk about us we...

things go right we...

one of us succeeds we...

one of us fails we...

Does this affect who you are now?
Do you want to keep or adjust these values and behaviours?

Your Next Choice

Put yourself first on page 63, or hold yourself high on page 132

Kindness

In the last week, how often did you show kindness?

Kindness to yourself:

Kindness to others:

What do these lists tell you?

Your Next Choice

Open your mind on page 131, or reflect on your Loop experience on page 153

Thank you

Make a list of things to thank your body for today – without it, you are stuck!

Your Next Choice

Loop back to re-evaluate your core on page 45

Turning points

What have been the key turning points in your life?
How would things be different without them?

Your Next Choice

Find what's missing on page 13, or go to page 134 to see yourself in a different light

Life-line analysis

Use the line below to draw out the peaks and troughs of life so far.
Are there any patterns? To what extent is this the visual you expected?

What contributes to the high points?

BIRTH

THE

And the low points?

How do you keep your head above the line?

Leave it there for now and move to...

Your Next Choice

Look for romance on page 109, or play games on page 121

Continue the line. What do the next ten years look like if you carry on as you are? What if you make changes? Draw out the two different lines. How much control have you got over the next ten years?

If you come past this page again, perhaps note here the one small thing you could do now to affect your life line in a positive way.

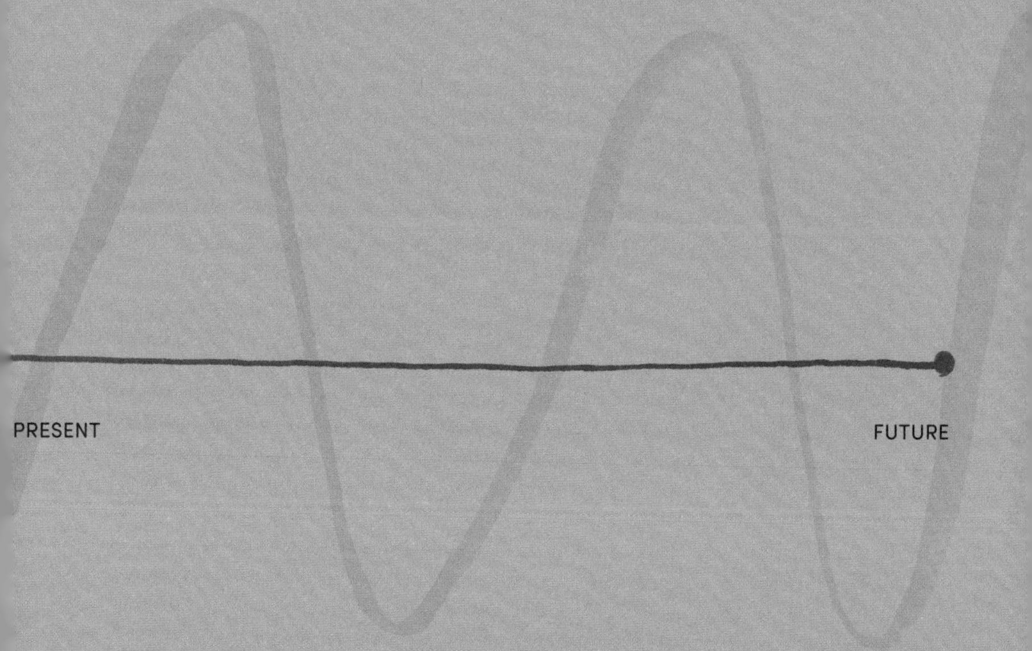

PRESENT

FUTURE

Your Next Choice

Be confident on page 51, or get nostalgic on page 117

Honesty

Give yourself a score out of ten for the following qualities.

	You	Boss
ORGANISATION	◯	◯
FORWARD PLANNING	◯	◯
SCHEDULING	◯	◯
PRIORITIZING	◯	◯
TEAM WORKING	◯	◯
INDEPENDENT WORKING	◯	◯
FOLLOWING INSTRUCTIONS	◯	◯
ASKING QUESTIONS	◯	◯

Would your boss or best friend agree?
Fill it in again as them

Are these all good traits?
Are any of them holding you back?

Your Next Choice

Loop back to something bigger on page 65

Time

Examine your current work habits by filling in this diagram to assess your day. How many hours does this circle represent? Work out the following proportions:

TIME SPENT ON TASKS

REQUIRED BREAKS

TIME SPENT ON OTHER ACTIVITIES. WHAT ARE THEY?

Are you happy with the result?

Your Next Choice

Take stock on page 82, or loop back to 115 to allocate your time

Different

How would your life be different if...

you had stronger relationships?

you believed in yourself?

you learned to let go?

you listened more, or listened less?

Your Next Choice

Make it different on page 75

Flip it

What really annoys you? Why?

Flip it

Now flip it!

The reverse shows you what you value. This means what is important to you is...

Your Next Choice

Be positive on page 18, or confront fear on page 142

Progress

Make two lists:

Things in my life that are helping me progress and grow:

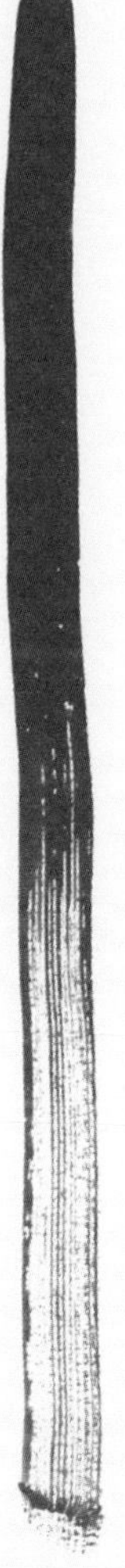

Things inhibiting or stopping my progress:

How much control do you have over each element in the right-hand column? Cross out anything you can't impact. What single thing could you do right now to make a difference to what is left?

Your Next Choice

Get advice on page 72, or interrogate time on page 114

Fulfilled?

Who or what has made you feel most fulfilled in the last year?
Where and when was it?

Your Next Choice

Explore your values on page 20, or consider narratives on page 119

When do you feel like someone has acknowledged your feelings? What do they do or say to demonstrate it?

How often do you do the same for others?

Your Next Choice

Ask for help on page 108, or visit page 147 to observe conflict

Gratitude

What are you grateful for today?

Now move to...

Your Next Choice

Write a not-to-do list on page 96, or visit page 122 for clarity

Use this space to write a thank you letter to someone. It could be for a great act of love or a small act of kindness. They might not know what it meant to you, so tell them. Now post it!

Your Next Choice

Move forward on page 31, or try reverse thinking on page 133

Forget

I would like to forget...

What didn't you write ?

Your Next Choice
Find satisfaction on page 104

All shall be well

"All shall be well, and all shall be well, and all manner of thing shall be well."
Julian of Norwich (English anchoress, 1343–1416)

Do you share her optimism?
What would all things 'being well' look like?

Your Next Choice

Take stock on page 27, or loop back to study time on page 115

Boundaries

What would you refuse to tolerate from a **friend**? Why is that the case?

What about from a **partner**?

How about from **work**?

How can you take these extreme examples and learn from them in your next interaction?

Your Next Choice

Loop back to page 95 and feel it out, or act on page 102

How do you feel about goal setting?

MOTIVATED

ENERGIZED

AMBIVALENT

PRESSURED

INSPIRED

ALIGNED

COMPROMISED

STRESSED

SOMETHING ELSE?

How has your past led to this?

Your Next Choice

Look beyond yourself on page 64, be dutiful on page 99, or find purpose on page 143

Ask yourself

Fill this page with questions to ask yourself and then consider answering them.

Your Next Choice
Express gratitude on page 34

Inner thoughts

What are all the things you thought today but didn't say? What would happen if you did?

Are there any you wish you had voiced? Why?

Your Next Choice

Loop back to say thank you on page 35

Becoming

"We become what we love and who we love shapes what we become."
Saint Clare of Assisi, Italian Saint (1194-1253)

What does love look like in your life?

Your Next Choice
Look at your phone on page 74

Social priorities

Your social media has been limited to ten followers: who are they?

You can only follow ten people: who are they?

Your Next Choice

Be brave on page 57, or try rose-tinted glasses on pages 110–11

What is at your core?

Look at the values below, then arrange them in the diagram. What do you notice?

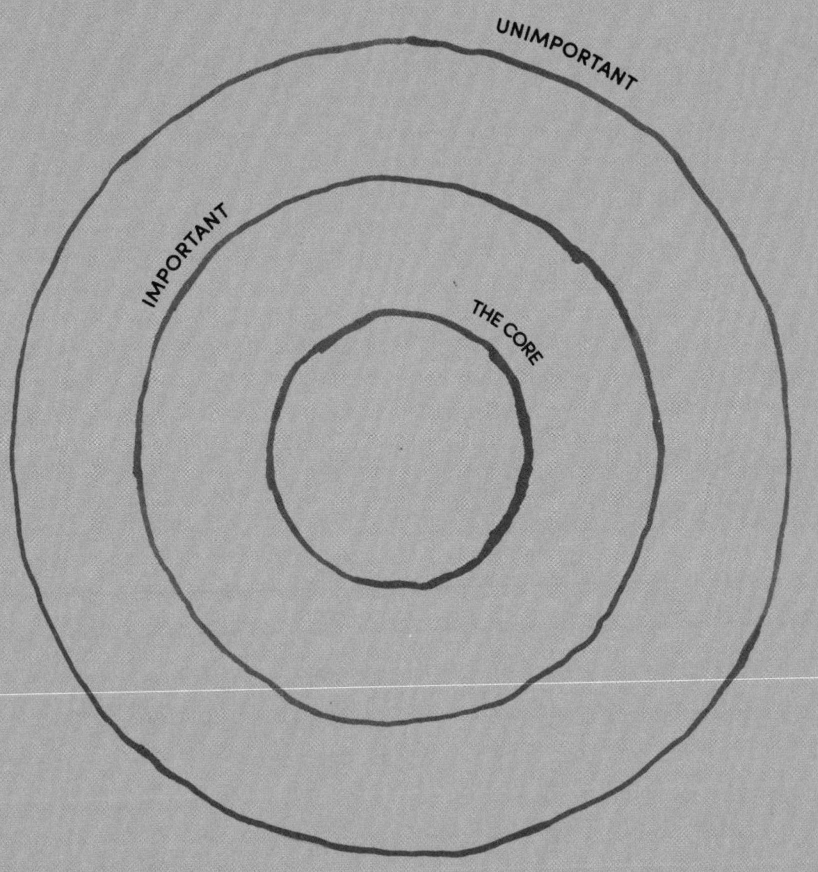

BALANCE	CREATIVITY	HONESTY	OPTIMISM	SELF-RESPECT
INDEPENDENCE	DETERMINATION	HUMOUR	POISE	SERVICE
COMPASSION	FAME	INFLUENCE	POPULARITY	STATUS
CHALLENGE	FAITH	KINDNESS	RECOGNITION	TRUSTWORTHINES
COMMUNITY	FRIENDSHIPS	KNOWLEDGE	REPUTATION	WEALTH
COMPETENCY	FUN	LEARNING	RESPECT	WISDOM
SUCCESS	GROWTH	LOVE	RESPONSIBILITY	
CONTRIBUTION	HAPPINESS	LOYALTY	SECURITY	

It's time to leave this page for now and move to…

Your Next Choice
Find your passion on page 14, or go to page 49 to discover what you believe in

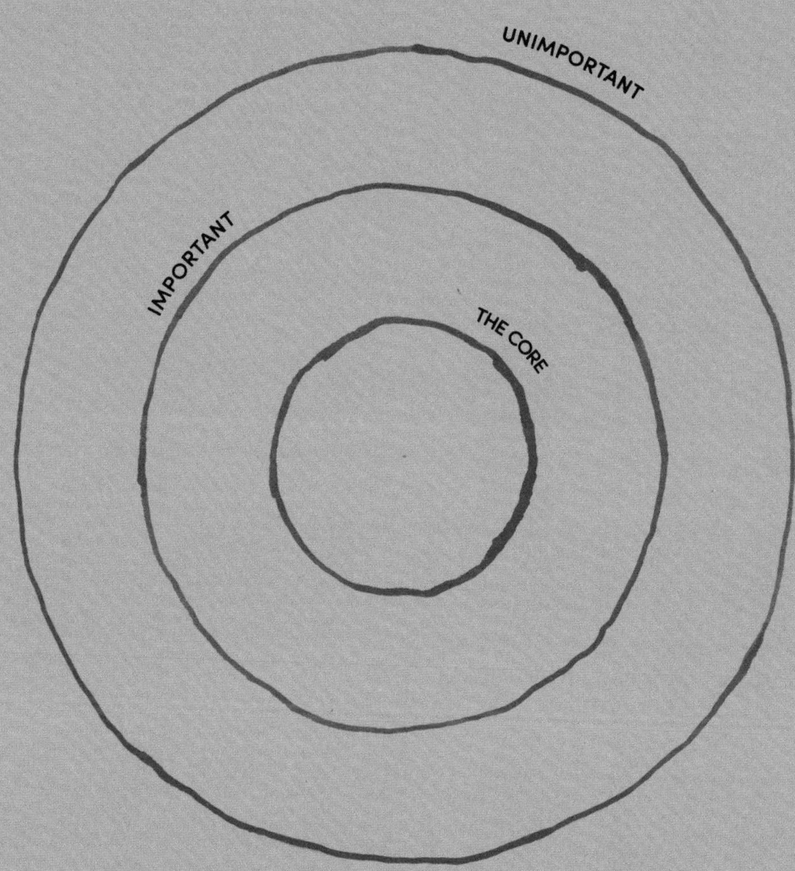

Consider this again from nother angle. If someone else was to fill in this diagram for ou, based on your actions this veek, what would it look like? re you presenting yourself in the way you wish to?

If you lived only by your core values, what would stay the same and what would change?

Your Next Choice
Try a backwards bucket list on page 10, or look back on page 93

I was taught that...

success is

education is

intelligence is

failure is

beauty is

fairness is

creativity is

difference is

power is

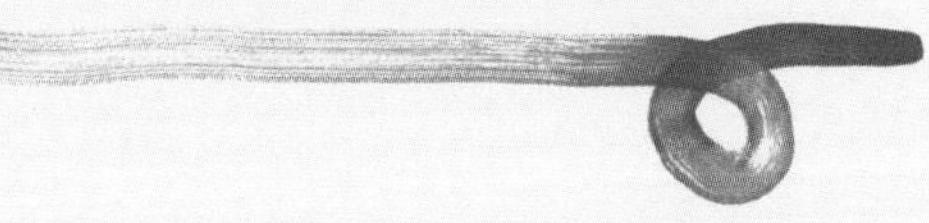

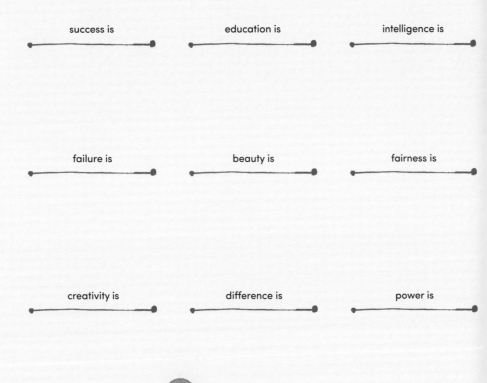

Not every lesson is valuable.
Which do you want to keep now you are an adult?
Which still have a strong influence?
How do you feel about them?

Your Next Choice

Loop back for a second opinion on page 55, or face your inner critic on page 61

Consumer

How many adverts did you see today?
Do you want what they are selling?

Your Next Choice

Be truthful on page 26, or discover what shapes you on page 81

Needs

Consider a close relationship you have. It could be with a friend, family member or partner. How aware are each of you of your own needs?

Your Next Choice

See it from another's perspective on page 54, or define quality time on page 113

Beliefs

What do you believe now that you would never have agreed with ten years ago? Try and convince the younger you.

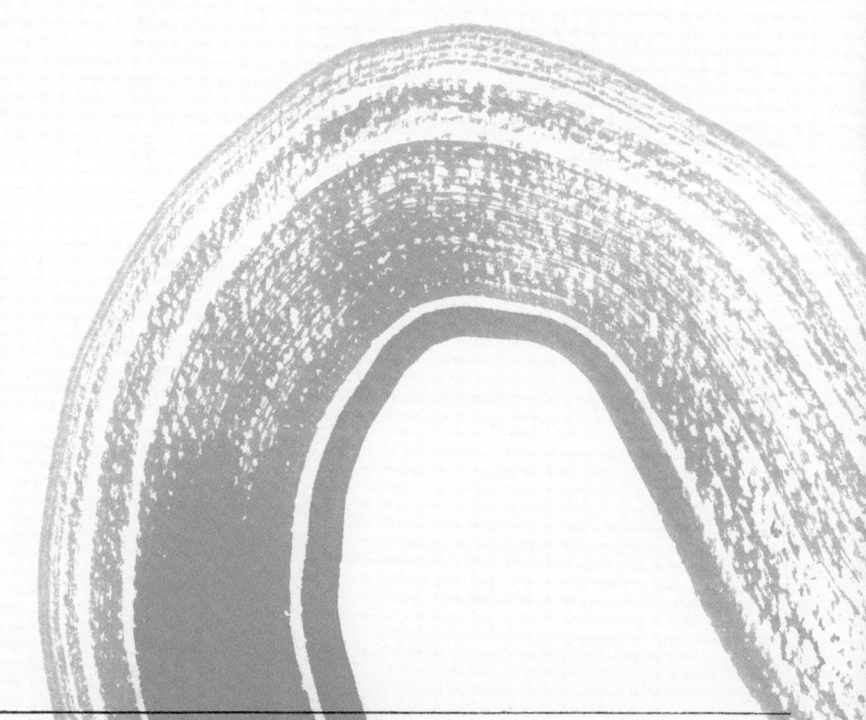

Your Next Choice

Find your flow on page 12, or get interested on pages 14–15

Feedback

Fill in these badges using feedback you've received in the last month.

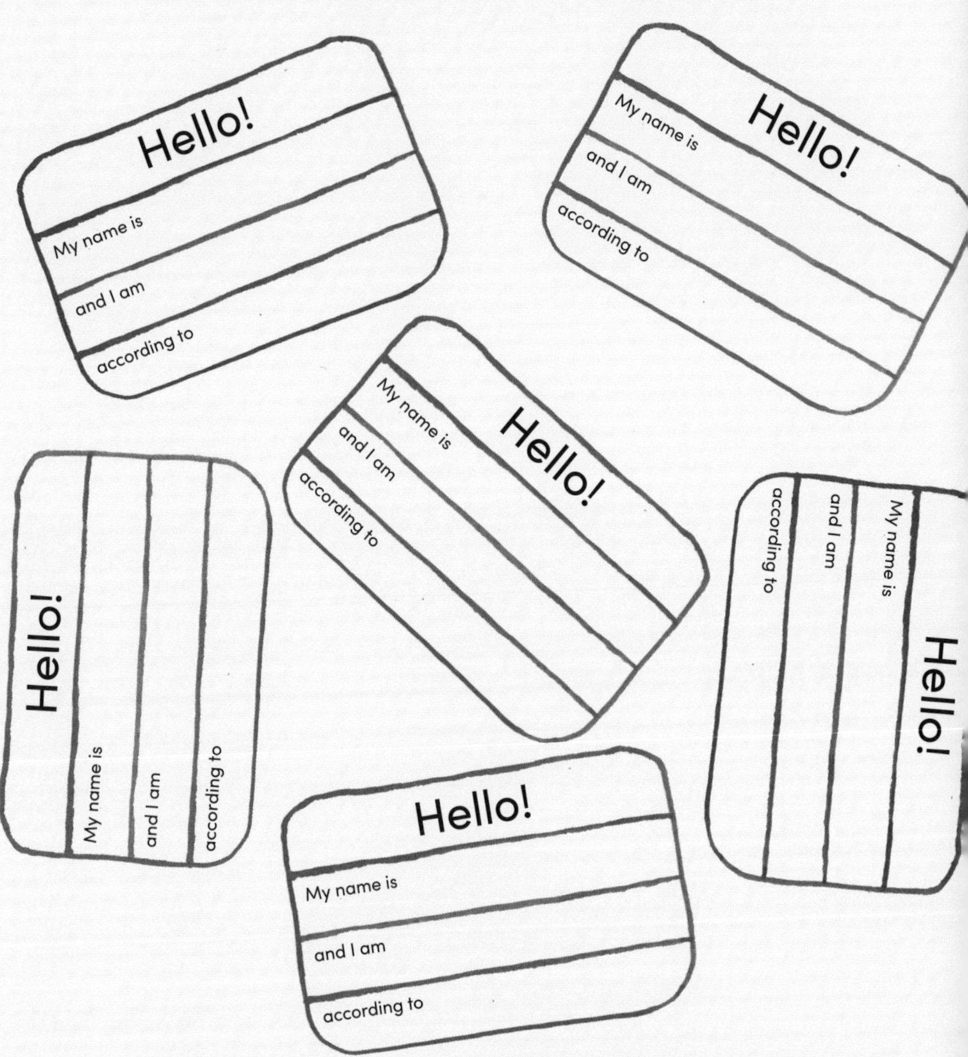

Which will you decide to wear? What do you notice about your choice?

Your Next Choice

Look at love on page 42, or stop wasting time on page 74

Self-confidence

Describe a time when you have been at your least confident.
Is there a positive statement that would encourage your past self?
How could this help you today?

Your Next Choice

Say yes on page 9, or think differently on page 28

Gut instinct

Our instincts are revealing. Complete the following sentences without too much forethought or self-censorship. You might want to add several endings to each sentence stem.

Kind people are... ________________

Sometimes I can't work because.... ________________

To be strong you... ________________

I never/always/sometimes say sorry because... ________________

I feel guilty about... ________________

My family think... ________________

It is better to be... ________________

than... ________________

because... ________________

I am proud of.. ________________

To be content is to be... ________________

I would never... ________________

Now choose one sentence from this list. What memories are linked to this idea?

Your Next Choice

Forget on page 36, or find satisfaction on page 104

Skill

If you could acquire a skill with no effort, which would you choose and why?
Would you tell anyone you hadn't worked for it?
What is stopping you from acquiring this skill now?

Your Next Choice

Loop back to your head, heart and hand on page 95, or act with purpose on page 102

Perspective

Use this page to see something from another's perspective. Choose an example of a minor conflict you had this week, perhaps at work or at home. What happened?

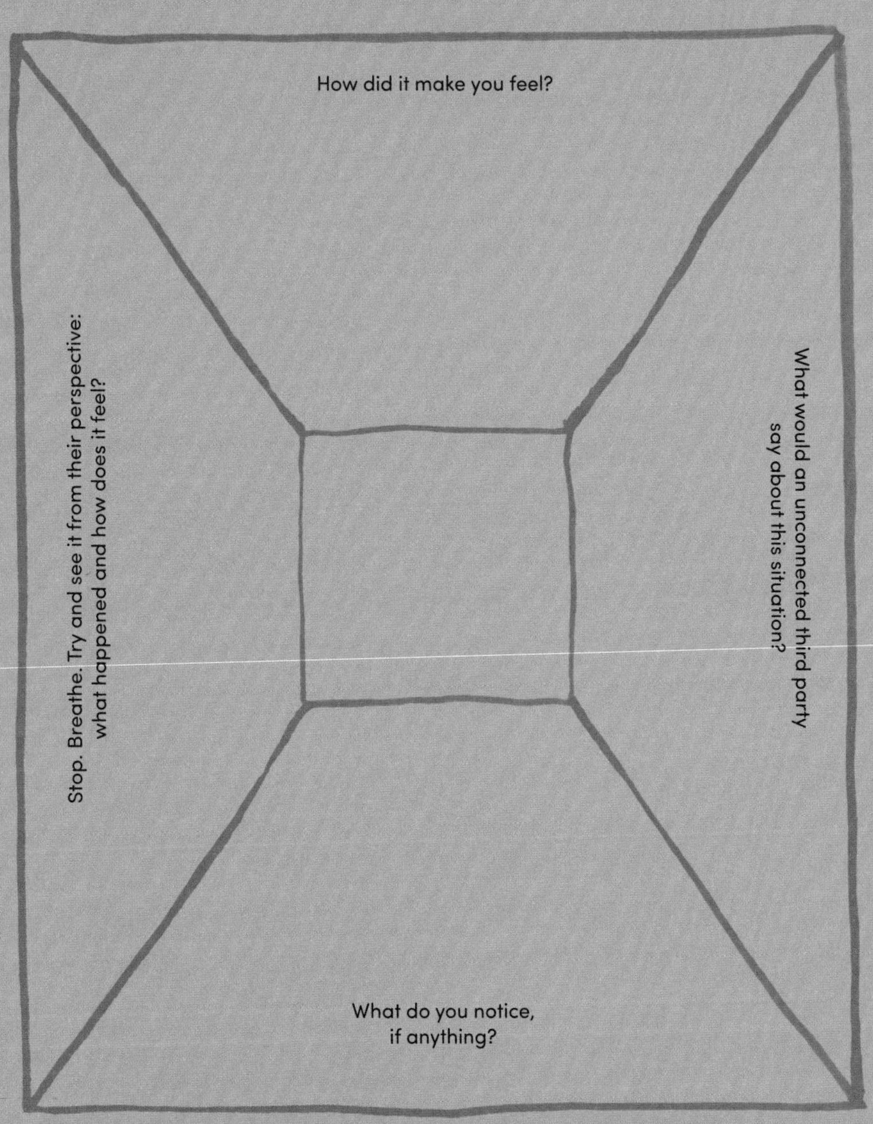

How did it make you feel?
Stop. Breathe. Try and see it from their perspective: what happened and how does it feel?
What would an unconnected third party say about this situation?
What do you notice, if anything?

Leave this here for now and move to...

Your Next Choice

Limit your followers on page 43, or empathize on pages 110–11

Hello again! Now that you're farther away from the conflict, do you see anything differently? How can you remember to see things from someone else's perspective? Scribble guidance to yourself here:

Your Next Choice

Trust the process on page 37, or challenge things on page 82

Fear

**When you are working, what scares you?
Would others recognize this fear in you? Why?**

Your Next Choice
Be guided on page 16, loop back and define satisfaction on page 105, or look within on page 123

Contribution

Imagine this shape is made up of responsibilities.
Which four factors have contributed to who you have become? (Upbringing, location etc.)
Assign each of them a portion of the shape, and explain it. Is this the same ratio you would like there to be in five years' time? Why or why not?

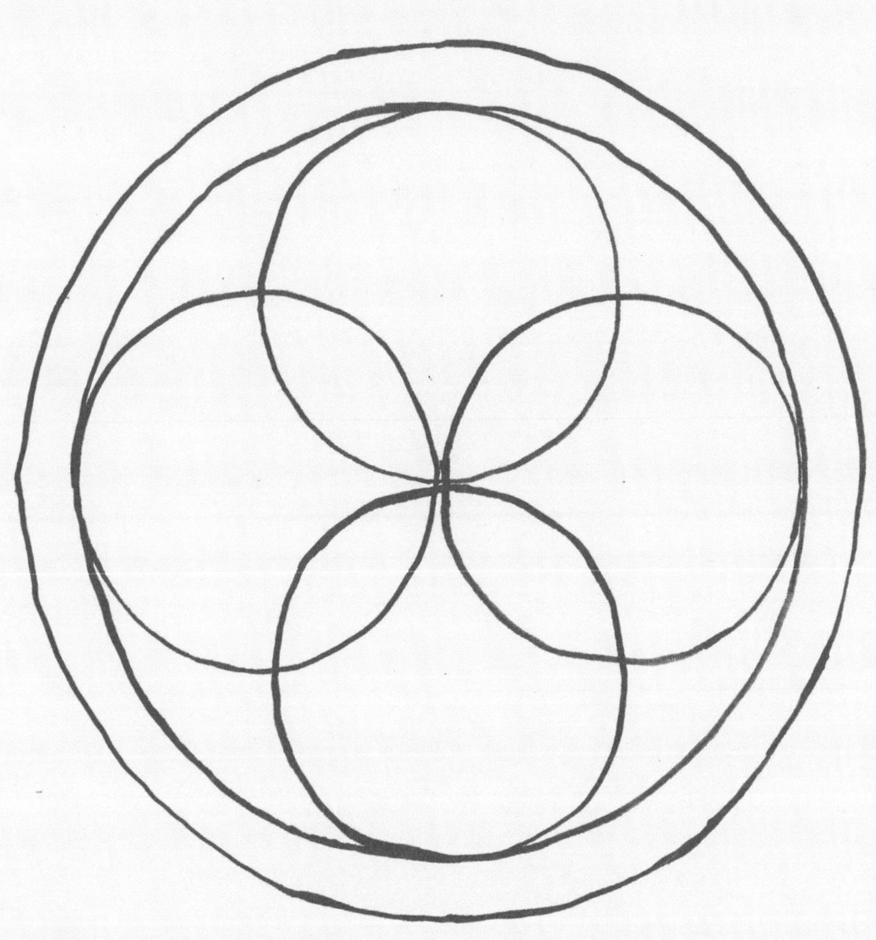

Your Next Choice

Loop back to express your needs on page 85

24 blocks

Here is your day divided into one-hour blocks. How did you use them?

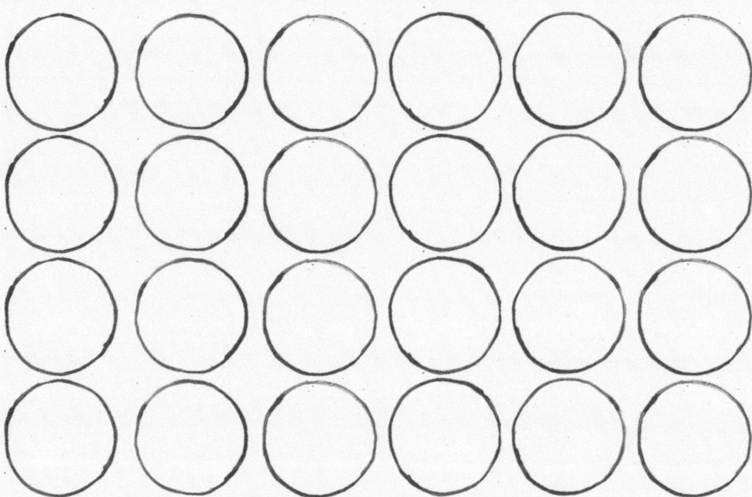

Here is tomorrow divided into one-hour blocks. How would you like to use them? To what extent is this a useful scheduling technique?

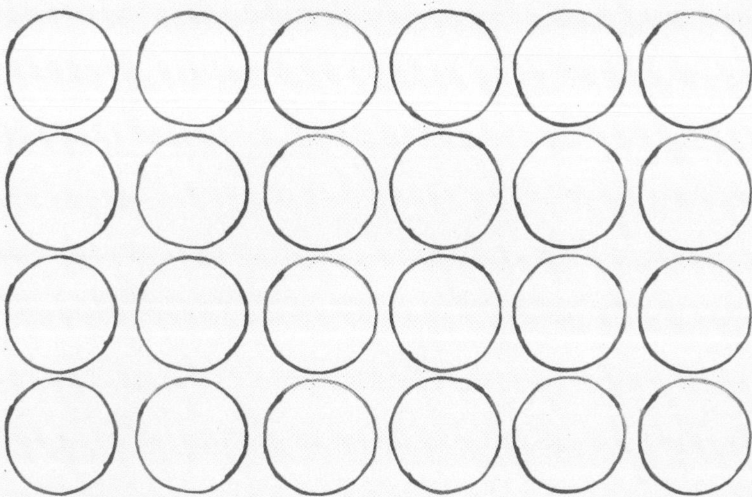

Your Next Choice
Find balance on page 124

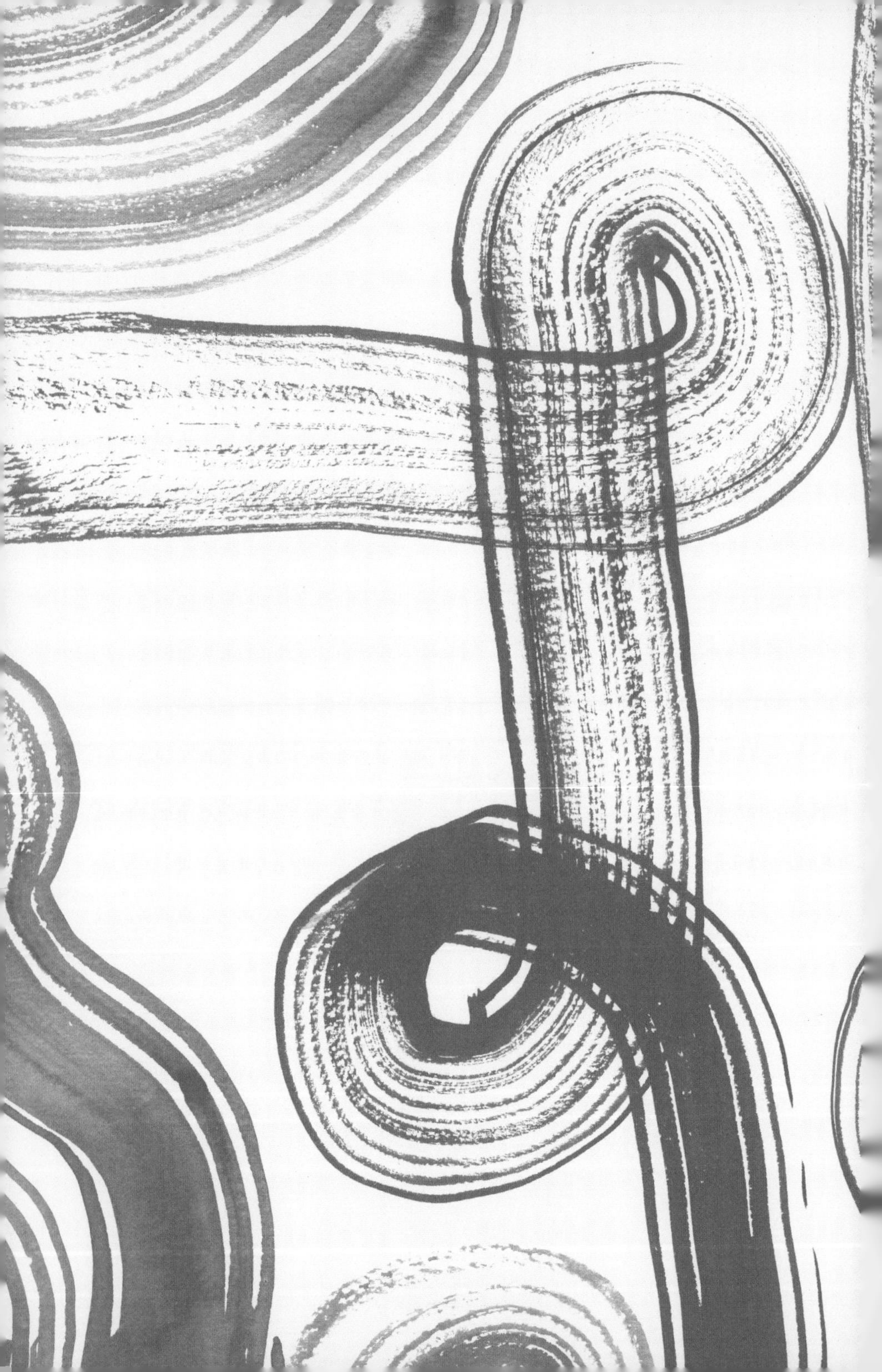

Check the evidence

Make a list of the negative things you tell yourself.
If you showed this list to a friend or family member, how would they contradict it?
What about a colleague or your boss?

What would it take for you to believe them?

Your Next Choice
Trust yourself on page 37

Yes and no

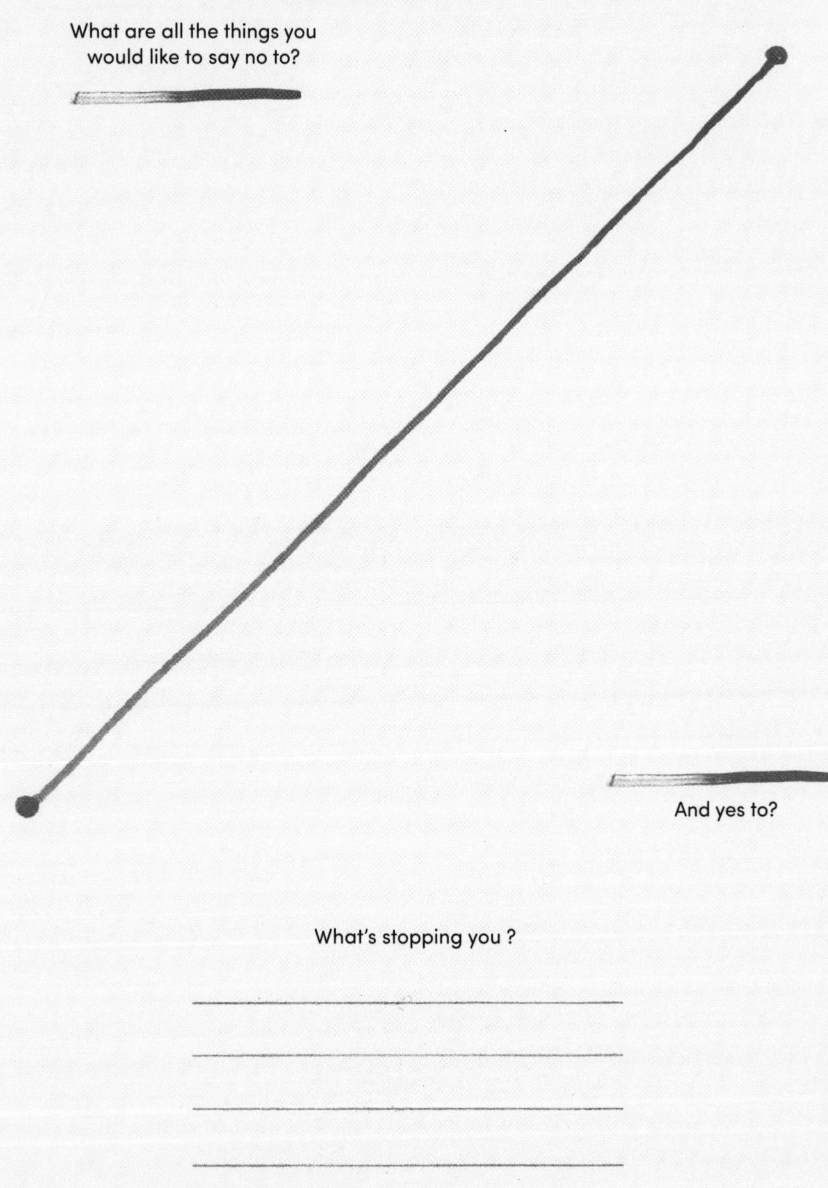
What are all the things you would like to say no to?
And yes to?

What's stopping you ?

Your Next Choice

Make progress on page 31, or take it on board on page 72

Oxygen masks

In an emergency situation, we are told to put our own mask on before helping others.

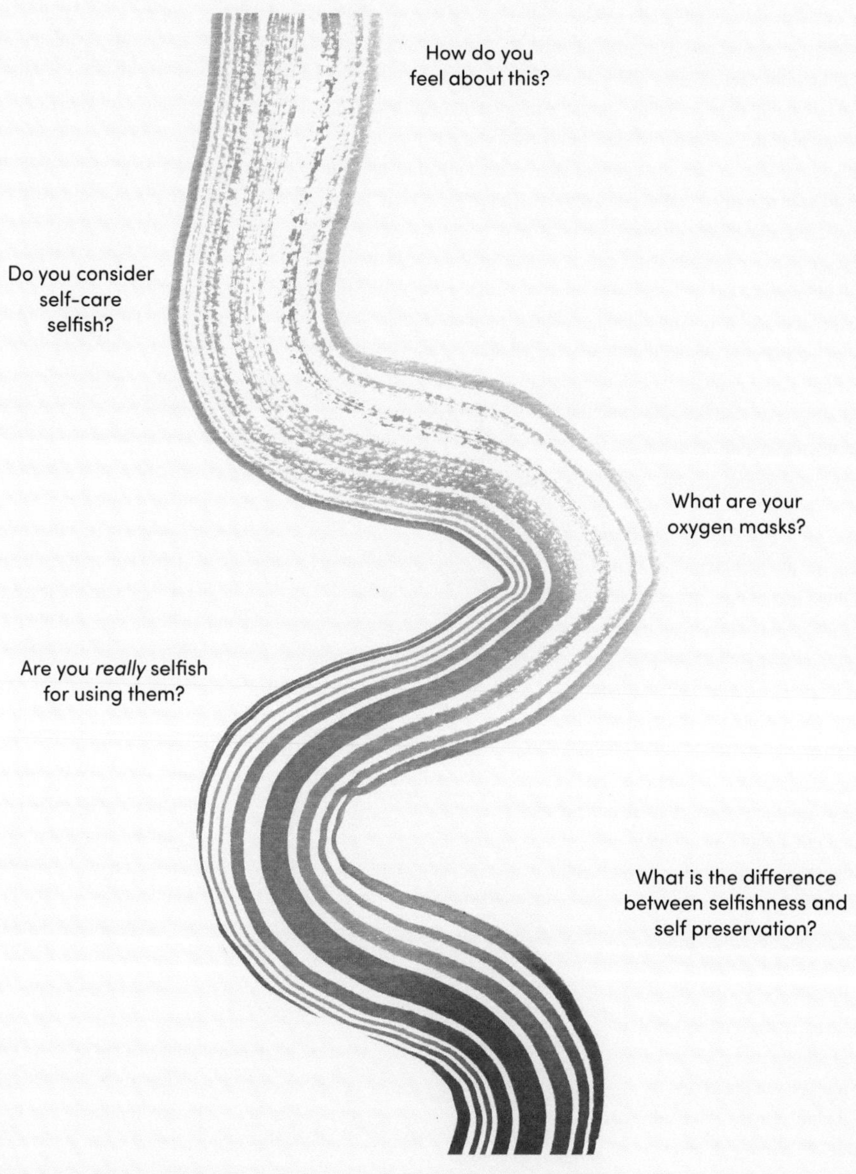

How do you feel about this?

Do you consider self-care selfish?

What are your oxygen masks?

Are you *really* selfish for using them?

What is the difference between selfishness and self preservation?

Your Next Choice
Examine your core on page 44, find certainty on page 130, or like yourself on page 132

Bigger than me

We are all drawn to the idea of something bigger or larger than ourselves. Sometimes we find it in religion, sometimes in an ambitious goal and sometimes in our relationships. Think about a time when your life felt meaningful. What were you doing and how did it feel?

Sometimes the way to find an answer is to identify all the 'wrong' answers. Think about a time when you felt really unaligned or distanced from your idea of meaning. What were you doing and how did it feel?

Leave it there for now and move to...

Your Next Choice
Focus on you on page 69, or tune into your intuition on page 150

Now you've looped back, re-read your answers on page 64.
Do these still resonate with you? Why or why not? Are you closer to finding meaning?

Still searching? Don't panic, it takes time. Try writing a summary of your life from the perspective of your grandchild, real or imagined. What can you see from this perspective?

Your Next Choice

Accept kindness on page 33, or seek support on page 108

Wishes

What do you wish you had time to do?
If you could change something now, what would it be and why?
What do you wish for your future self?

Your Next Choice

Discover how you process emotions on page 94, or experiment on page 129

Louder

What would speaking up have looked like for you today?
How would it have felt?

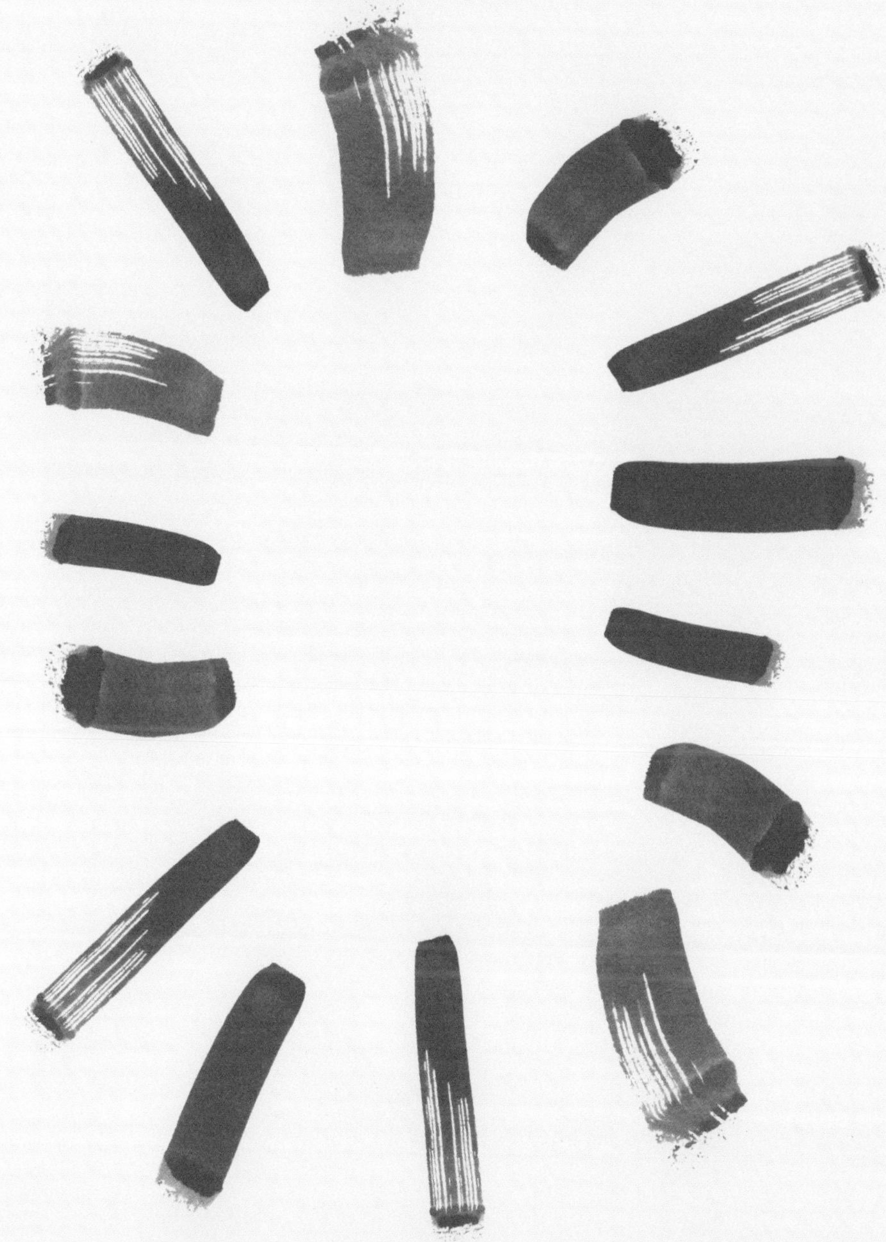

Your Next Choice

Consider what has shaped you on page 58, or loop back and be bold on page 85

Conflict

Often the true cause of conflict lies deeper than what is immediately apparent on the surface. Consider an ongoing or recent argument, then ask yourself five 'whys' to try and determine the root cause:

Why are you in conflict?

Why is that?

Why is that the case?

Why do you think that?

Why?

Now make a plan to resolve it: what should happen first?

Your Next Choice

Locate your missing pieces on page 13, or examine pivotal moments on page 23

I am

Complete these phrases with just one word.
Go with your gut instinct, don't overthink it.

I am ______________________ My work is ______________________

My body is ______________________ People are ______________________

The past was ______________________ The world is ______________________

My heart feels ______________________ The future is ______________________

My home is ______________________

What do your responses tell you?

____

____

____

Your Next Choice

Find your current state on page 97, or work out what matters on page 120

Thought experiment

Everything your own is taken from you for a week.
You can have one thing back each day. What do you choose first? In what order would you like the rest of your belongings returned? What does this tell you?

Your Next Choice

Experience life without failure on page 98, or make decisions on page 140

Dead drawer

There are some things we just don't want to think about.
What would you like to put in the dead-thoughts drawer?
File it away and leave it alone. It's done.

Your Next Choice
Set boundaries on page 38, or gain a skill on page 53

Advice

What's the best piece of advice you have received from your family?
Could it be of use now? How?

Your Next Choice
See time differently on page 114

Confidence

I am at my most confident when…

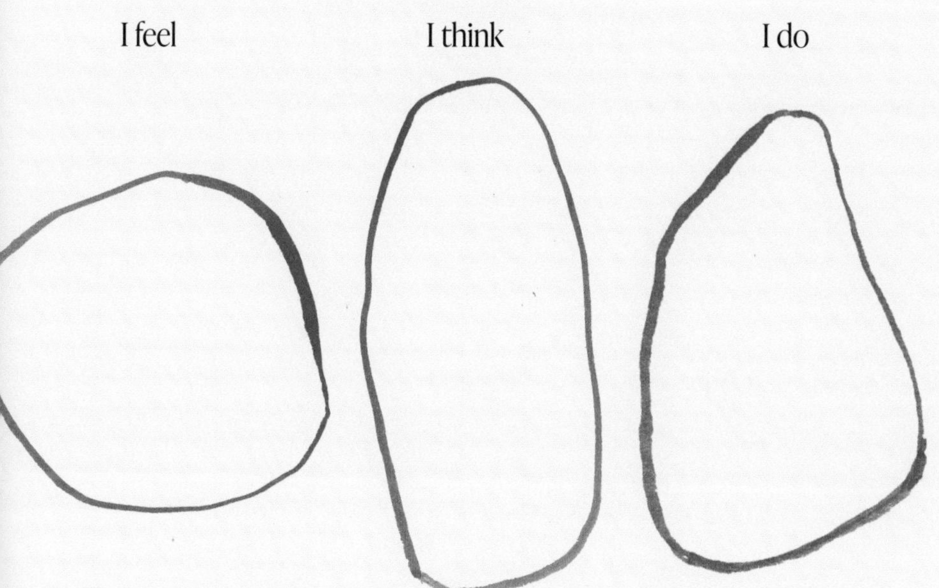

Which element is most powerful in securing your ongoing confidence?
What can you do to hold on to your confidence?

Your Next Choice

Find purpose on page 39, or responsibility on page 99

Do something different

1. List all of the apps on your phone – or other distractions.
2. Now plot them on the quadrant. (If they are time well spent and make you feel good, they go in the top right quadrant.)

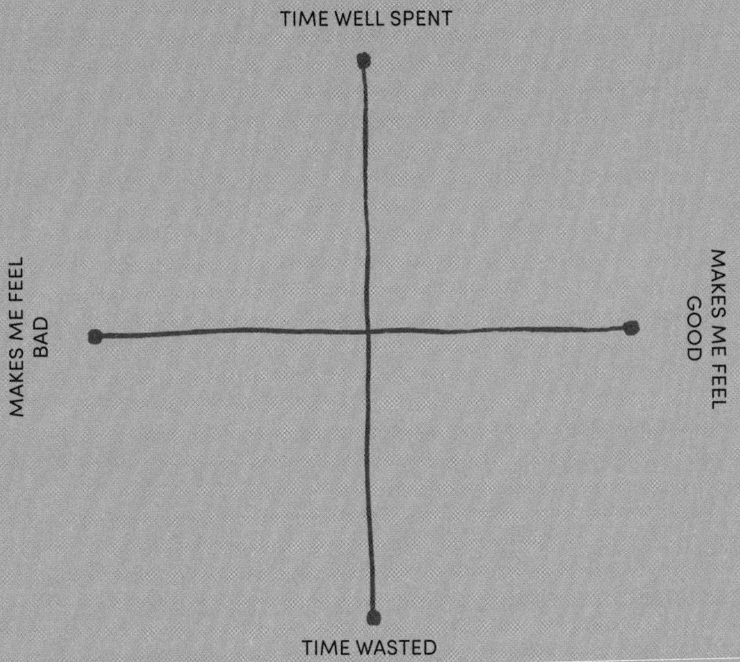

Now use the grid to decide what to delete from the time-wasted zone. The one you waste the most time on proceeds to the next round.

__________ VS. __________

__________ VS. __________

__________ VS. __________

DELETE THIS ONE: __________

Now on to your next choice...

Your Next Choice

Know thyself on page 19, or consider consumption on page 81

You're back! What are all the things you did instead of using this app?
Did you manage to delete it permanently? What impact did your choices have?

Your Next Choice

Be open-minded on page 131, or evaluate personal space on page 139

Distance

Imagine conducting your close relationships 10,000 miles apart.
How do you do that? Which would be worth the extra effort?

Your Next Choice

Determine your life's path on page 24

What matters?

What matters more?
Choose your answer and explain your choice:

BEING GOOD,
OR BEING THE BEST?

NOVELTY
OR VALUE?

TRYING AND FAILING,
OR NOT TRYING AT ALL?

ADVENTURE
OR SECURITY?

HARD WORK,
OR NATURAL TALENT?

KNOWING YOU'VE DONE A GOOD JOB,
OR OTHERS KNOWING YOU HAVE?

CREATIVITY
OR LOGIC?

DOING YOUR DUTY,
OR CHALLENGING CONVENTION?

TIME
OR MONEY?

PLANNING
OR SPONTANEITY?

FRIENDS
OR FAMILY?

WHAT MATTERS
TO YOU ?

Your Next Choice

Discover your interests on pages 14–15, or make a change on page 127

Free flowing

When do you feel at your most free?
What comes easily to you?

Your Next Choice

Loop back to page 145 to rethink feedback

Self-image

What could you learn from observing yourself tomorrow?

Your Next Choice

Take a closer look at your family on page 20, or satisfaction on page 32

Influence

What did you consume this week?

I READ

I WATCHED

I LISTENED TO

I SCROLLED THROUGH

I BROWSED

Which made you happy?
Which made you sad? Why?

Your Next Choice

Look at yourself differently on page 19, or loop back to something bigger on page 65

Contribution

Rarely is a conflict all one person's fault. Rather than assigning blame, consider instead how you, others and the environment contributed to it.

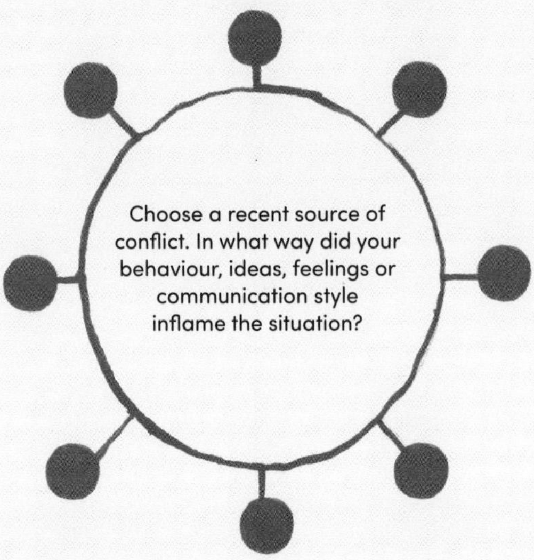

Choose a recent source of conflict. In what way did your behaviour, ideas, feelings or communication style inflame the situation?

How did other people contribute to it?

What about the environment?

How might this help defuse future conflicts?

Your Next Choice

Loop back to set time limits on page 115

Brave and strong

"Even in a world that's being shipwrecked, remain brave and strong."
Hildegard of Bingen (mystic, 1098–1179)

What shipwrecks are you navigating?
How can you stay strong?

Your Next Choice
Say thank you on page 34

Assertiveness

Sometimes it is hard to say what we want and need without coming across as aggressive or uncaring. It can help to write a script in preparation.

Describe the situation:
this is how I see it...

Describe your feelings:
this makes me feel...

Identify your needs:
I need you to...

Name the consequences:
so that this can happen and this won't happen.

Leave it there for now and move to...

Your Next Choice

Look at life's momentous moments on page 23, or examine discord on page 68

It's time to go deeper. Why does expressing your needs feel confrontational?
We let other people do it all the time!
Practise saying what you want and need here.

I want	I feel	I need

Now, for balance, be empathetic and
recognize another's wants and needs in a certain situation:

They want	They feel	They need

How does that feel? When would you find this easy or
challenging to do? Why is that the case?

Your Next Choice

Say no on page 90, or be kind on page 126

Unfinished

Sometimes conversations end unsatisfactorily and feel unfinished.
Write a letter to someone to finish that conversation.

Your Next Choice

Loop back to re-evaluate your work–life balance on page 125

What if?

What if every internet search you did cost a penny?
Where should the money go? How would it alter your habits?

Your Next Choice

Allocate time on page 59, or find balance on page 124

Rescue

Do you save yourself or wait to be saved?
Why is that?

Your Next Choice

Trust your intuition on page 41, or limit your contacts on page 148

No!

It can be hard to say no, at work and at home.
One technique is to pre-empt it. What would you like to say no to?

On a scale of 1–5 how likely are you to?

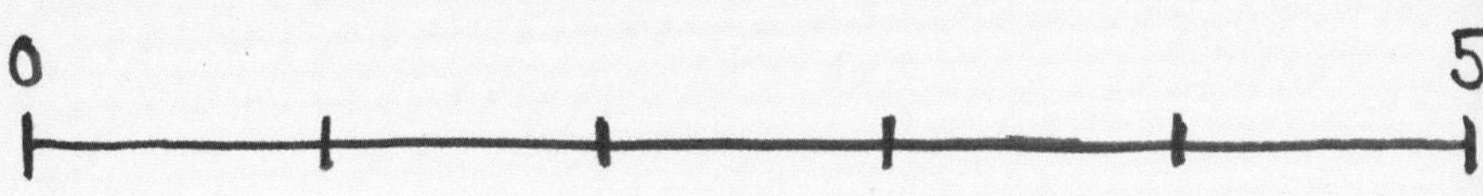

Why is that?

Make a list of ways in which you could say no.

Choose one from the list, then rehearse it before you go into the conversation.

Your Next Choice

Forgive on page 116, or loop back to attain equilibrium on page 125

Love

"Don't forget love, it will give you all the madness you need to unfurl yourself across the universe."
Mirabai (poet, c.1498–c.1547)

What do you really love?

Where will it take you?

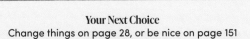

Your Next Choice

Change things on page 28, or be nice on page 151

Spinning plates

Exactly how many plates are you spinning?
List them in small groups.

Do some need to smash? Can you hand some over?
Can others be ignored for a while?

Your Next Choice

Focus on love on page 42, or listen to feedback on page 50

History

If you were a book,
what values would be in your prologue?

What did your upbringing
give you?

Consider the first few chapters.
What values appear there?

And now, in real time,
how will it end? What will you have learned?

Your Next Choice

Believe in yourself on page 137, or loop back to reconsider constructive feedback on page 145

Head Heart Hand

Self-reflection is a messy and complicated business. You are a brilliant mix of so many things, people and experiences. You also probably prefer a certain way of processing emotions or events. Which of these speak to you?

Head

Ruled by thought, logic and processing. Tend to theorize first, act later. Try to see the world as logical and predictable.

Heart

Learn by experience and reflect on feelings. Test the emotional consequences or feelings associated with decisions before acting. Relationship-led.

Hand

Act first, think later. Test through doing. Try first, reflect, then try again.

I tend to lead with the head/heart/hand because...

____

____

____

____

The strengths associated with this approach are...

____

____

____

____

The negatives are...

____

____

____

____

It's time to leave this spread and move to...

____

Your Next Choice

Reflect on your self-image on page 80, or look at lasting impressions on page 119

On your second visit to this spread, look at how you defined your preferences. Imagine that other people in your life are answering these questions for you. What would they say? Choose one of the following to explore how others might perceive you. My boss/colleague/peer/teacher/family member/partner/friend/acquaintance/stranger/neighbour...

would say that I lead with the head/heart/hand because....	would say I am at my best when...	and at my worst when...

In reality, we are a combination of all three.
However, it is interesting to explore how you see yourself.

Your Next Choice

Be self-assured on page 128, or say what's on your mind on page 141

Not-to-do list

Write your not-to-do list here. What necessary tasks do you no longer do because you delegate or outsource them, or because you consider them to be unimportant?

Now, add the things you want to say no to, followed by the things that are actually someone else's responsibility.

How do you feel about your not-to-do list?

Your Next Choice

Forget on page 36, go with your gut on page 52, or imagine your highest self on page 103

Nourish

What do these words mean to you: functioning, well, stable, thriving, nourished, nurtured, flourishing, surviving? What are you like in each state? Which state are you in now? Is that where you like to be?

Your Next Choice

Question yourself on page 40, be strong on page 83, or find meaning on page 120

Endless possibilities

What would you do if you knew you could not fail?

What would happen if you tried?

Your Next Choice

Loop back to your core values on page 45, or be decisive on page 140

Duty

When was the last time you did something you didn't want to do? What was it and what made you do it? To what extent was this duty, obligation or something else?

Your Next Choice

Look at the bigger picture on page 64, or set goals on page 143

Mistakes

If you kept making the same mistake, what would you want someone to do about it? How do you feel about communicating mistakes to others?

Your Next Choice

Make yourself heard on page 84

Great acts

What is the greatest act of kindness you have received?
How did it feel?

Your Next Choice

Loop back to process on page 95

Highest self

What does it mean to be your highest self?
Write for ten minutes with this question in mind.

Your Next Choice

Forget on page 36, or be instinctive on page 52

Life satisfaction chart

Rate your satisfaction in the following areas by providing a score from one to ten (one being the lowest):

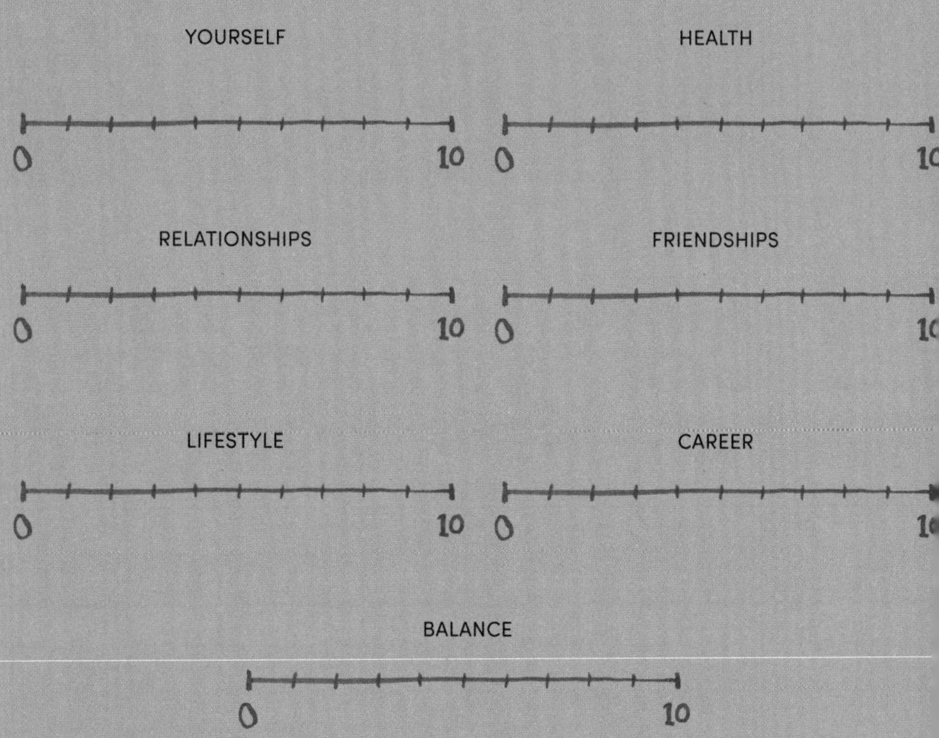

What do you notice?

That's all for now. It's time to move to...

Your Next Choice

Find work-life balance on page 124, or imagine a different way of seeing on page 146

Hello again. How did you measure satisfaction when completing page 104? Try to define what satisfaction means to you and where those ideas came from. Do any need amending?

Your Next Choice

Think big on page 98, or make decisions on page 140

Self-talk

Most of what I have said today has been...

positive/negative/
neutral

This is/is not what I expected
of myself because...

Those listening to
me might think...

This is accurate/false/
misrepresentative because...

Are you happy with what
your words are projecting?

Your Next Choice

Loop back to see it from the other side on page 135

Listening

When you talk, how much do you listen?

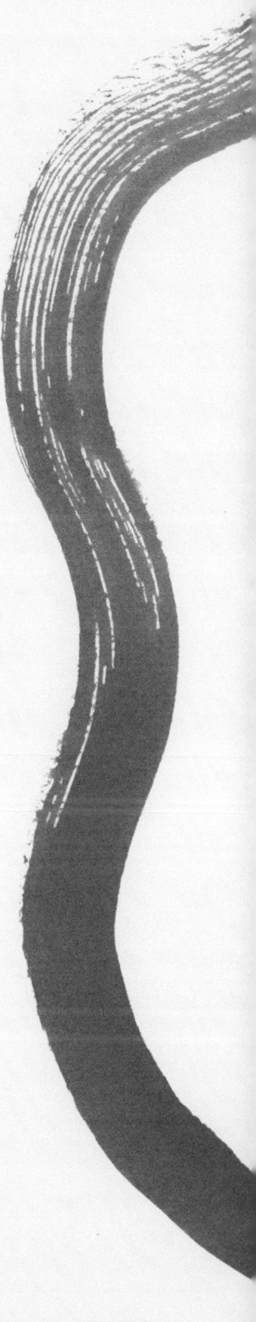

Your Next Choice

Speak up on page 67, or loop back to be bold on page 85

Help!

When was the last time you asked for help?
How did it feel?

Your Next Choice

Find hope on page 11, or examine conflict on page 147

Romance

In your opinion, what are the ideal traits of a romantic partner?
How do you measure up against your own list?

Your Next Choice
Reflect on feedback on page 144

Empathy

Choose an event and consider it through different spectacles.

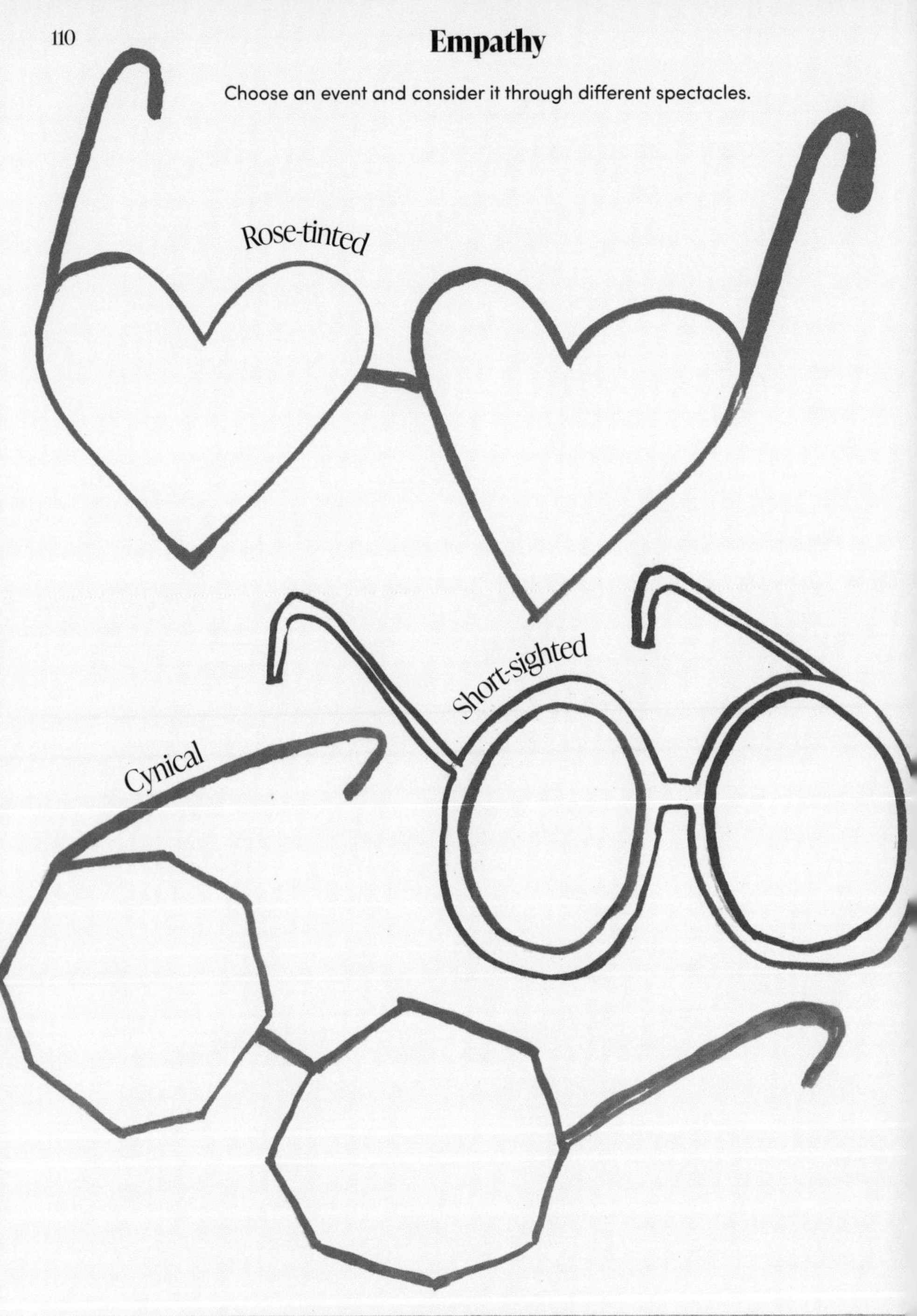

Your Next Choice

Face your fears on page 57, work out what's important on page 70, or try a different form of 'you' on page 123

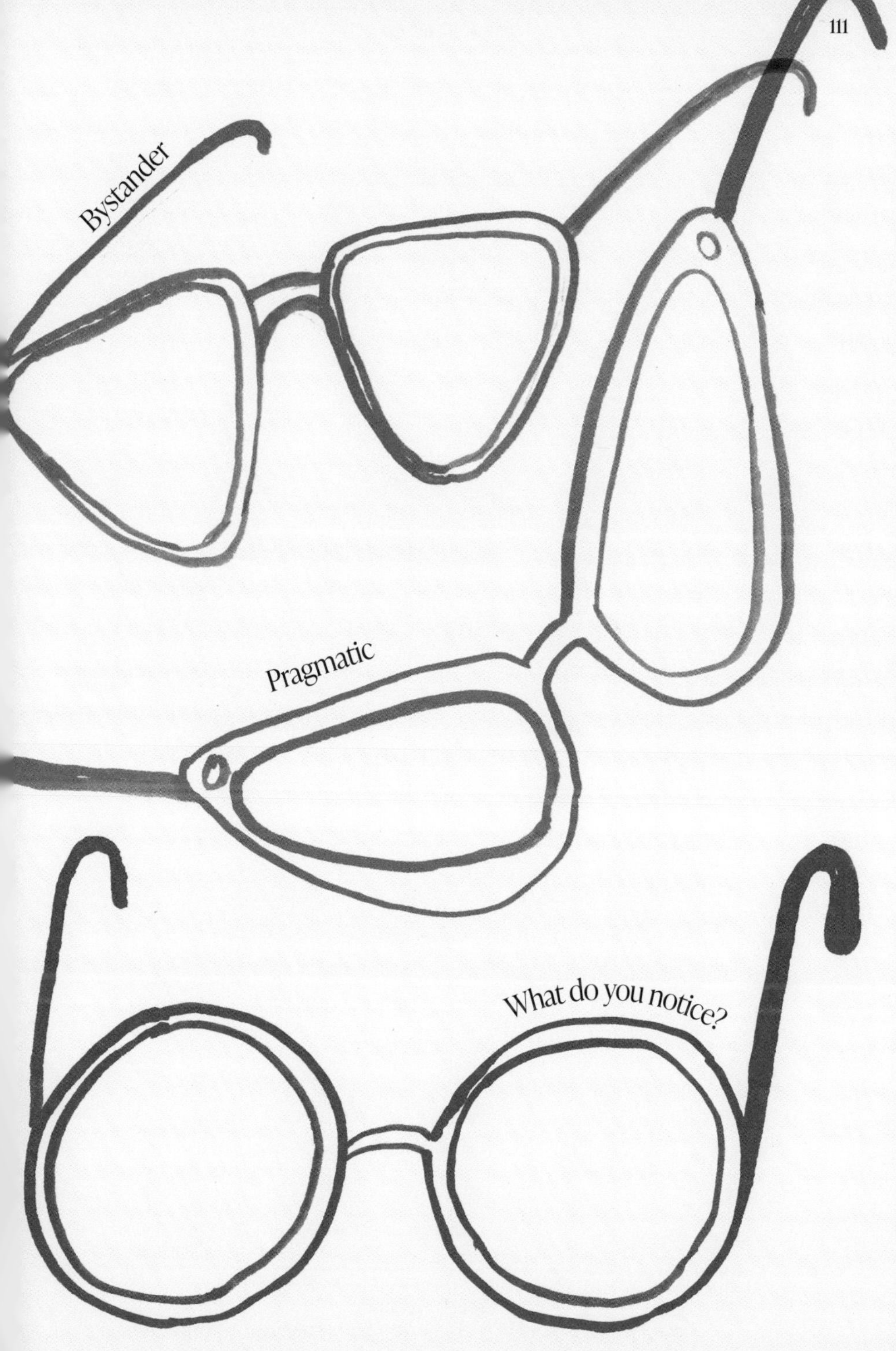
Bystander
Pragmatic
What do you notice?

Power of words

When was the last time someone's words made you cry? What happened?

What had the most effect: *what* they said, *how* they said it or *who* said it?

Having reflected, how do you feel about this now?

Your Next Choice

Look at how you respond on page 94

Quality time

How would you define the following types of time?

Novelty	Negative	Productive

What is the current balance in your own life?
Are you happy with it?

Your Next Choice
See it from their side on page 54

168

There are 168 hours in a week. Look, they're all here.
Shade in the amount you need for sleep.
Now look at what's left: how many are for work? Home? Socializing? You?
What can you fit in?

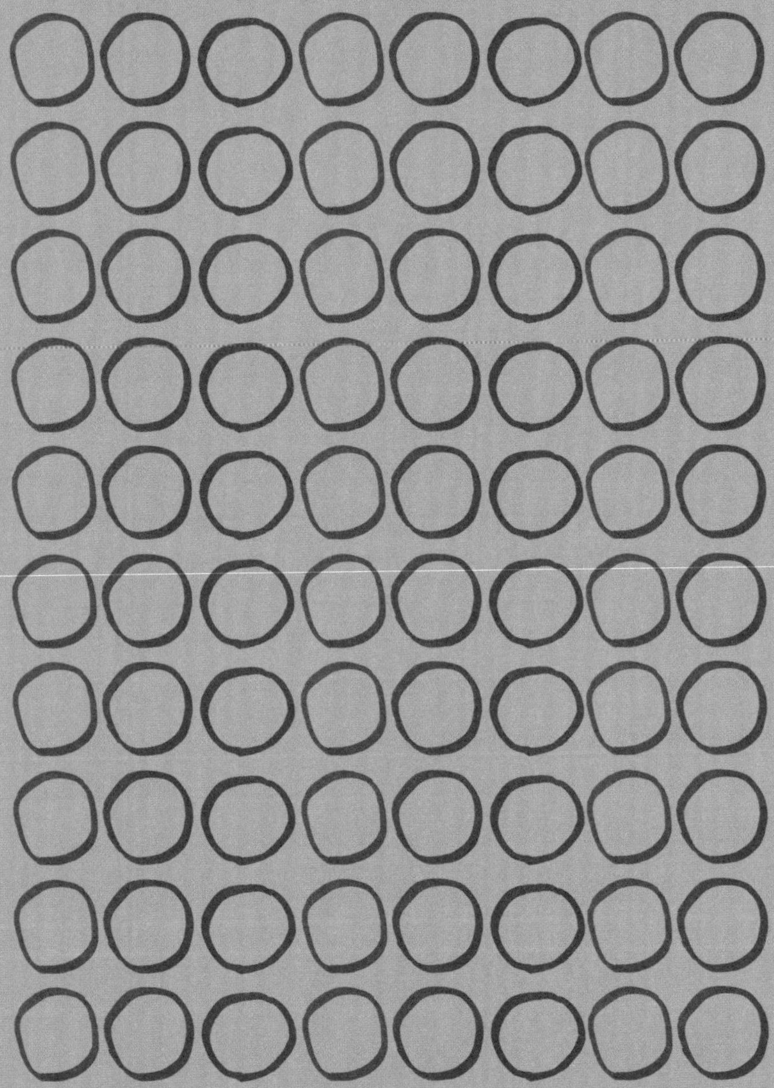

Your Next Choice

Perform a relationship health check on page 48, or change your perspective on page 54

Which allocations would you like to increase or decrease?
How will you use these hours instead?

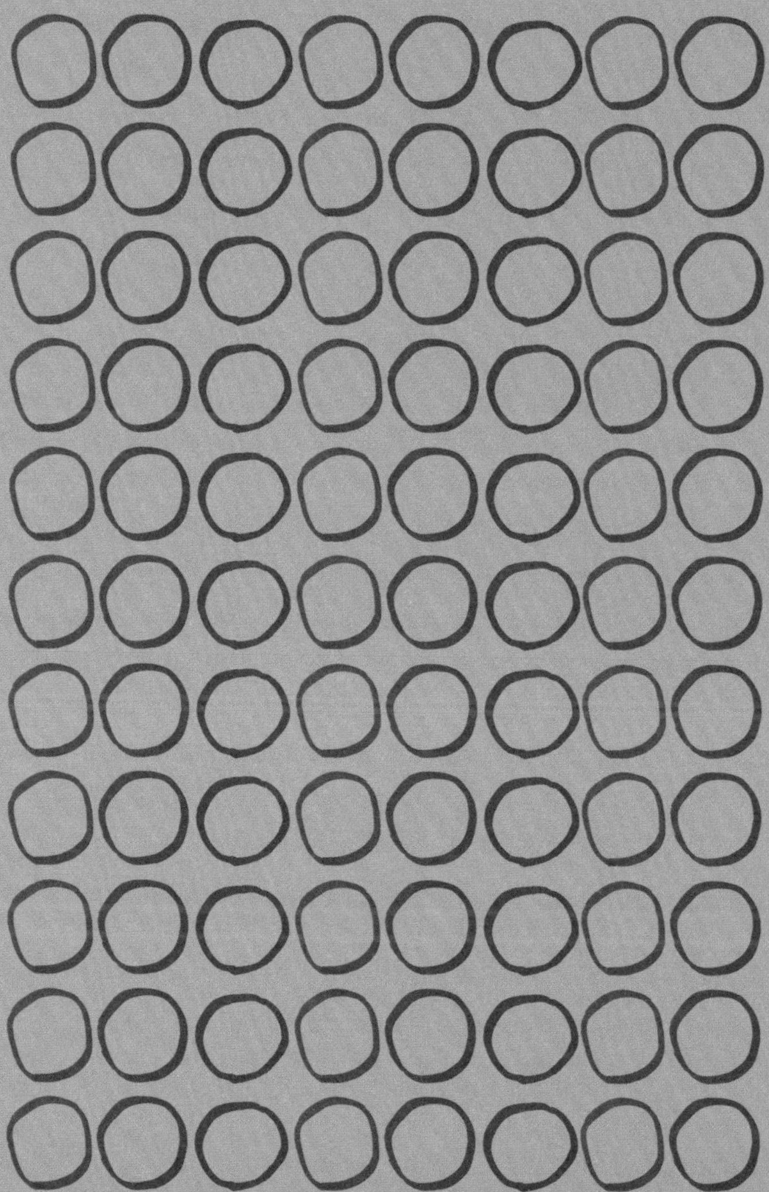

Your Next Choice

Experience positivity on page 18, or happiness on page 136

Forgiveness

How will you forgive others this week? How will you forgive yourself?

How does this empower you?
How does it hold you back?

Your Next Choice

Find peace on page 86, or loop back to achieve equilibrium on page 125

Nostalgia

Is there any advice you wish you'd given yourself five years ago?
What has enlightened you since then?

Your Next Choice

Listen to your inner monologue on page 106,
or loop back to see your strengths differently on page 135

Imprints

Experiences, people and emotions leave lasting impressions. What has left its mark on you? Record some of these things here. What was the experience, in brief, and what effect did it have?

What didn't you write? Why?

Your Next Choice

Examine family ties on page 20, or practise self-care on page 63

Importance

What is important?
Write alongside the spiral, noticing the prompts as you go.

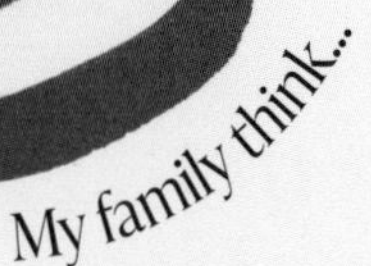

My friends think...

I think...

Your Next Choice
Give thanks on page 34, or ask questions on page 40

Mind games

If you could grant one piece of wisdom to all newborn babies, what would it be and why? How would the world change because of it?

Your Next Choice

Be romantic on page 109, or receive feedback on page 144

Vision

Fill in the graph below. It could be how you feel or think or what you do. It could be external goals or internal desires. Or all of them!

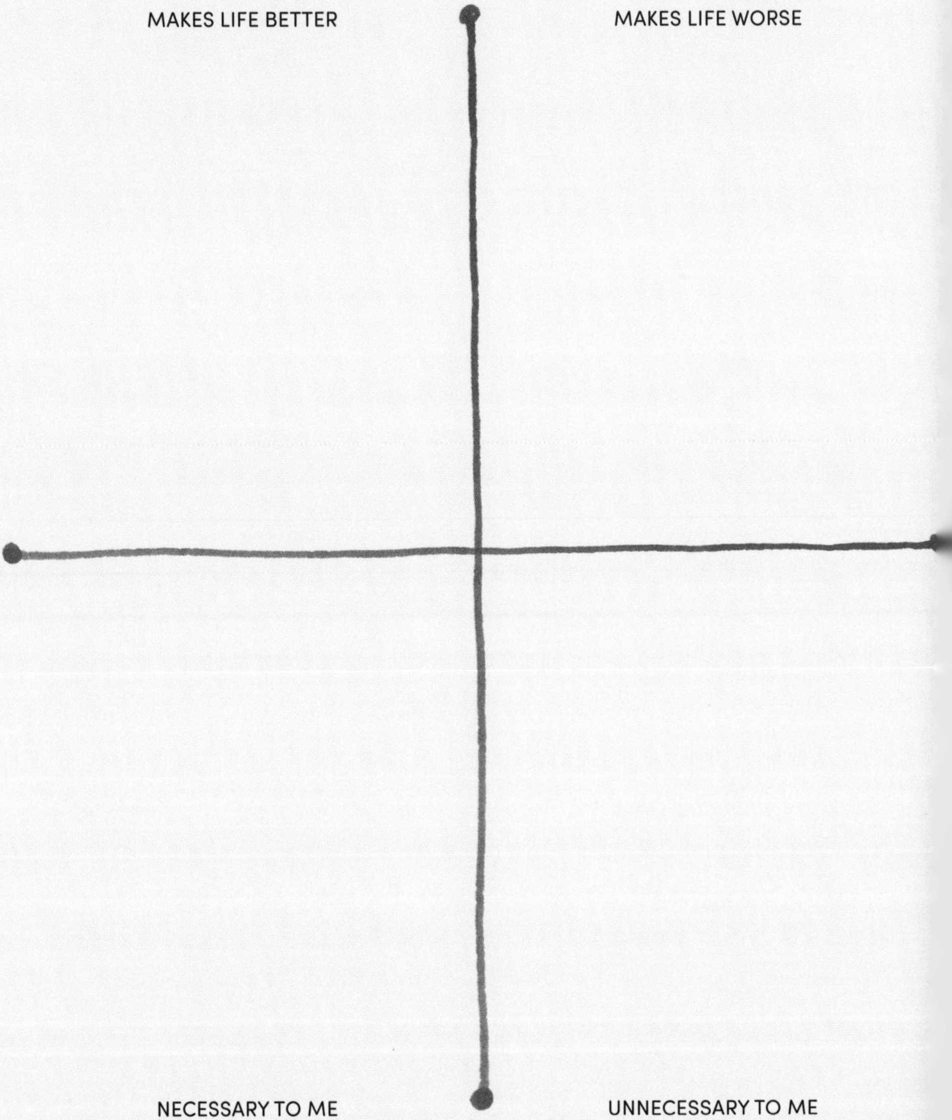

MAKES LIFE BETTER

MAKES LIFE WORSE

NECESSARY TO ME

UNNECESSARY TO ME

Your Next Choice

Prioritize on page 96, or find your highest self on page 103

Insight

Think of a time during the last month in which you acted in a very 'you' way. What were your other options? Why don't you try taking them and see what happens?

Your Next Choice

Meet your mentors on page 16, or loop back to find satisfaction on page 105

Balance

Look at the diagrams below. If each shape represents life and work, which pairing reflects the balance you have, and which captures the balance you want?

Look at them again, and answer as your partner, friend, family or boss. How do those answers compare? Complete these sentences:

Ideally, I would like the balance of life and work to be...

____

____

____

Realistically, I think it has to be...

____

____

____

In the long term, I hope...

____

____

____

Leave these shapes for now and move to...

____

Your Next Choice

Receive feedback on page 50, or task manage on page 92

Looking at these diagrams again, what are the consequences of your current arrangement? What would you stand to gain or lose if you changed this?

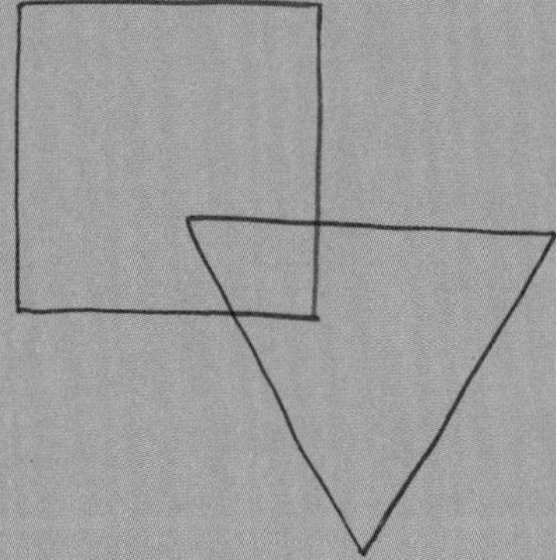

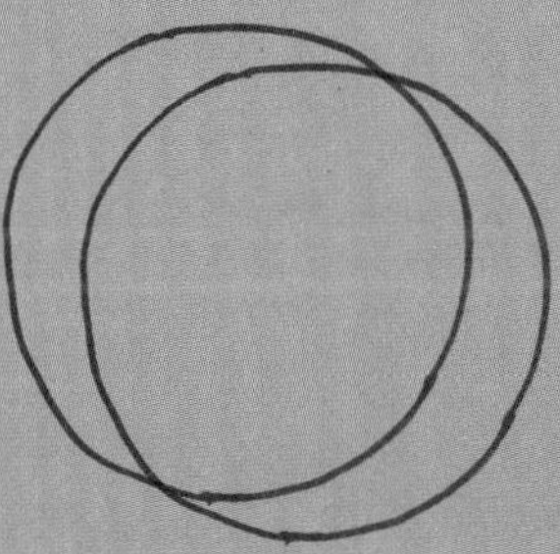

Your Next Choice

Reflect on life lessons on page 46, or complete an imaginary diary on page 149

Being kind

When you are in pain, physical or mental, what are the kindest things you can do for yourself? What stops you from doing them?

Your Next Choice
Practise saying no on page 90, or 'I forgive you' on page 116

Change

How does the word change make you feel – excited, intimidated or indifferent?

Your Next Choice

Set goals on page 39, or consider confidence on page 73

Self-belief

What threatens your inner confidence and self-belief? What strengthens it?
How can you protect your sense of self?

Your Next Choice

See mistakes differently on page 101, or push yourself on page 141

Life in a box

Imagine there's a box underneath your bed. Choose five items that represent your life as it is now to place inside it.

What do you hope will be in there when you retire?

Your Next Choice
Find out who leads on page 94

Trust

To what extent do you trust yourself?
Is this more or less than you trust others?

Your Next Choice
Get centred on page 44

Open mind

Life is so much richer when we keep an open mind. Practise flexibility by choosing a fundamental principle that you agree with, like 'hard work always pays off', then use this page to argue the opposite! How does it feel?

Your Next Choice

Reflect on your Loop experience on page 153

Self-regard

Do you like who you have become?

Your Next Choice

Focus on values on page 44, or trust on page 130

I can't
(cross out the 't'...)

Circle all the things you can't do.

Talk to new people/think of new ideas/
be creative/solve problems/give a presentation/be spontaneous/
be organized/manage money/keep to a budget/concentrate/
look after my physical health/exercise/eat well/care for those around me/
make others happy/be on my own/be with other people.

Now for each of the things you have circled, find a piece of evidence from your life that contradicts this.

Your Next Choice

Say yes and no on page 62, or look at your week on page 114

Two-sided

We mistake weaknesses for wholly negative traits, but they can actually tell us about our strengths. For example, 'I never speak up in meetings', is very close to, 'I listen carefully to what others say before responding'. What are your weaknesses? How could you turn them into strengths?

Take that power and move to...

Your Next Choice

Listen to your intuition on page 41, or save yourself on page 89

Take a moment to re-read page 134. Guess what? Your strengths can hint at your weaknesses, too. For example, 'I really care about the outcome of a project', can easily become, 'I'll feel like a failure if my project fails'. Which of your strengths could become weaknesses? How can you protect yourself?

Your Next Choice

Empower your past self on page 51, or work out what you love on page 91

Happiness

Write down four words that mean happiness to you.
Do the same for success, balance and fulfilment.
What do you notice about your words?

Your Next Choice

Flip it on page 30, or live in better conditions on page 142

I can

Complete this sentence as many times as possible.

I can ______

I can ______

I can ______

I can ______

I can ______

I can ______

I can ______

I can ______

I can ______

I can ______

I can ______

I can ______

I can ______

I can ______

I can ______

I can ______

Your Next Choice

Eschew perfection on page 17, or find freedom on page 79

Personal space

What characterizes your setting: both your physical and emotional space, and your geographical area? Describe them here.

Which do you value most?
Which, if any, would you like to change?

Your Next Choice

Show tenderness on page 21, or reflect on your Loop experience on page 153

Decision making

Choose an event from this week that required you to make a decision and act on it. Higher stakes are best. What happened? Describe it below.

How did you make your decision? Were you most influenced by your heart, hand or head? What would have happened if you had allowed another part of yourself to make the decision?

Your Next Choice
Appreciate your body on page 22, or loop back to zoom in on page 45

Anything else?

What's on your mind?
Anything else?

Your Next Choice

Be assertive on page 84, or reflective on page 101

Face your fears

"Fear is the cheapest room in the house.
I would like to see you living in better conditions"
Hafiz (poet, c.1320–1390)

What scares you?
How can you improve the conditions in which you live?
Set a timer and write for ten minutes.

Your Next Choice
Loop back to look forward on page 25

Purpose

I feel purposeful when...

Does anything get in the way?

Your Next Choice

Tune into the big picture on page 64

Feedback

We get feedback all the time, but it is hard to actually hear it; we tend to ignore the positive and get defensive about the negative. Take some time to consider what people said to you today and how you reacted.

Personal praise

Professional praise (skills, effort or outcomes)

Which did you most value and why?

Own that feedback with pride and move to...

Your Next Choice

Build boundaries on page 38, or find peace on page 71

Let's think more about feedback. When we get constructive feedback, or negative comments, we usually have an emotional response. This can be helpful and healthy, or the total opposite. List the constructive feedback you have received this week.

Does who it's from make a difference?	How did you feel at the time? And a week later?	How do you decide whether or not to listen?

Your Next Choice

Assess your make-up on page 58, or pay attention on page 107

Imagine

For a whole day, you can only see either words or pictures. Which would you choose, and why?

Your Next Choice

Divide your day on page 59, or focus your energy on page 88

Conflict

Generally speaking, there are four categories of communication in conflict...

Direct aggression:

bossy, personal, overbearing, explicit.

Indirect aggression:

sarcastic, ambiguous, manipulative, deceitful.

Submissive:

passive, victimized, wailing, apologetic.

Assertive:

direct, responsible, spontaneous, honest.

How would you categorize the people in your life? Add their names to the relevant column. Where would you put yourself? What do you notice?

Your Next Choice

Be positive on page 11, or find distance on page 76

Contact

You can only have five contacts in your phone.
Who are they and why?

Your Next Choice
Loop back in recognition on page 35, or listen carefully on page 41

Diary

Think of five diary entries you have never written but wish you had.

Your Next Choice

Learn lessons on page 46, loop back to re-evaluate conflict on page 55, or silence your inner critic on page 61

Intuition

Develop your intuition by giving time and space to these two questions, simply letting your mind focus and your pen move for ten minutes.

What is really going on?

What do I need to know?

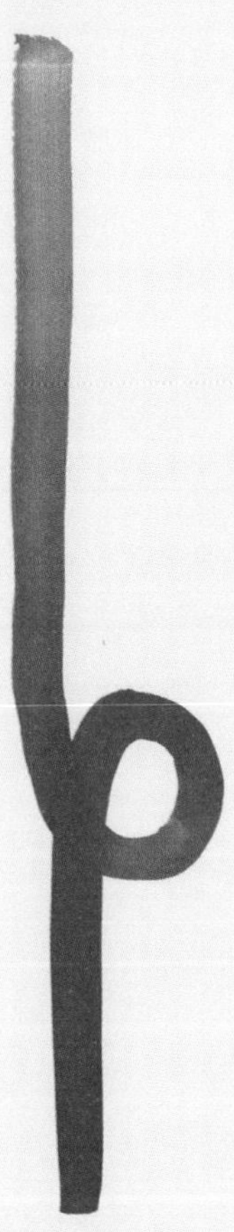

Your Next Choice

Work out who you are on page 69, nourish yourself on page 97, or find value on page 120

Pay it forward

Five nice things that I could say today are...

I am likely/unlikely to do so because...

I think the other person would think....

Your Next Choice

Be self-confident on page 51, or loop back to reflect on change on page 75

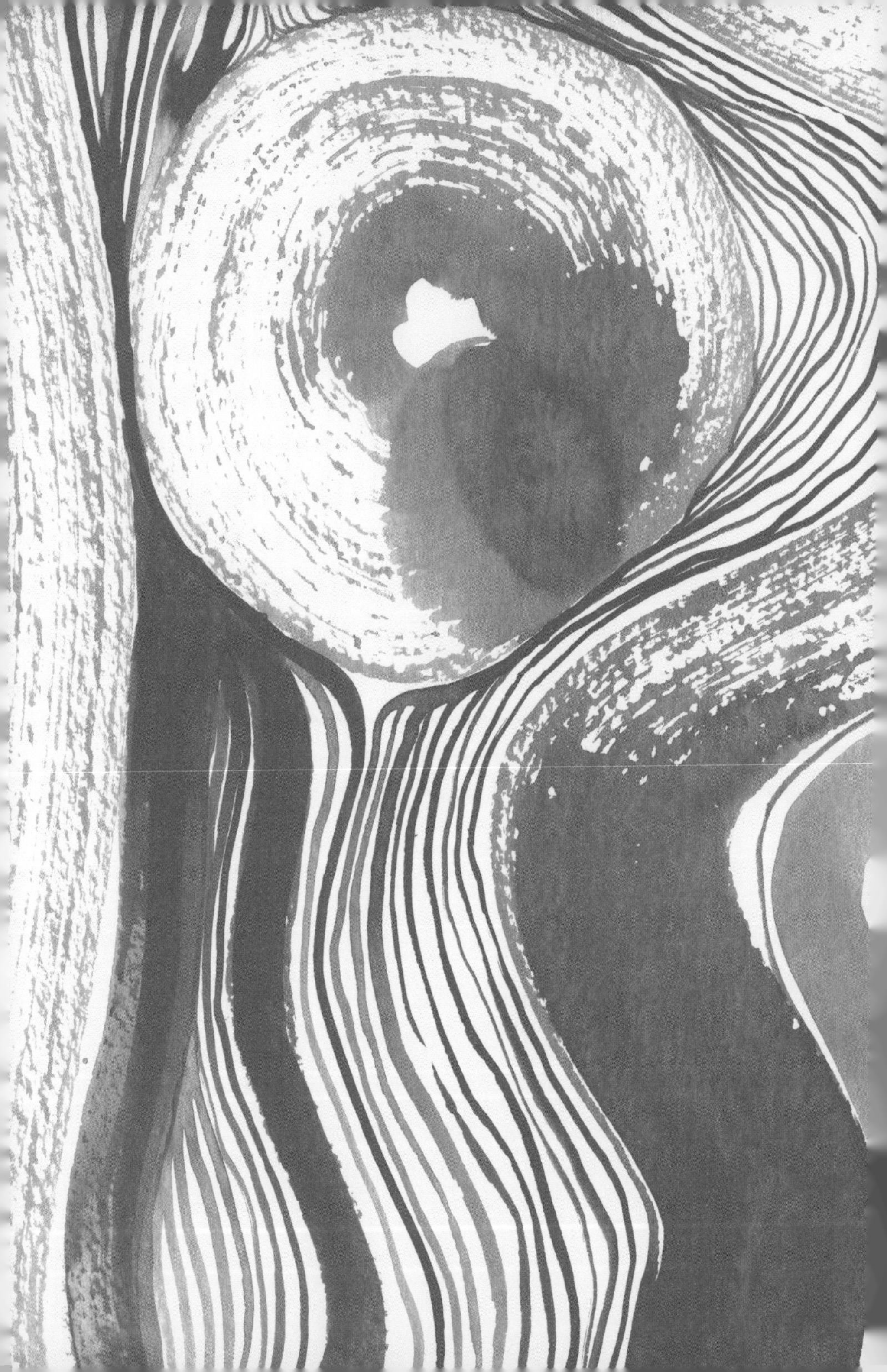

Where are you now?

You have come to the end of this journal, but not of your growth.
Take a moment to reflect on your experience of Loop.

Was the journey as you expected?
Why or why not?

If you could speak to yourself
as you filled in the first page, with all the benefits
of hindsight, what would you say?

Reflect on the act of journaling.
In your Loop, what core ideas and themes
did you keep returning to?

What have you learned,
and what will you take with you?

What's next?

This journal is full of your thoughts, wishes and plans. Its pages contain your reflections and your loops. Its conclusion, therefore, is entirely and utterly yours. Your journal is different to anyone else's. Different in content, obviously, but just as importantly, different in its path. Your route through the journal is unique.

Your journal is a valuable resource. Each page contains reflections on your actions. Loop's content is very telling. It reveals who you are right now, and what you need next. At this moment, the content of the journal is at its most beneficial. What will you do with it?

One of the most beautiful things about your journal is how completely 'you' it is; each of the four threads has revealed the complete picture of what makes you, you. Every time you consider your influences, you get a clearer picture of who you are. This provides a greater ability to know what you want and how it may be supported or sabotaged by yourself and others. This journal will have helped you to become more self-aware and more empowered to express your voice.

I challenge you now to take this self-knowledge and transform it into action. What do you have to lose? What do you stand to gain? The end of this process is a good time to make pledges and plans. What happens next is up to you.

Whether your Loop is a work of art or a collection of scrappy notes isn't important. Re-read it, recycle it or put it on a shelf. It doesn't matter what happens to it: after all, its content is only indicative of where you are right now. Continued growth is what matters next.

Loop's ongoing value lies beyond the page. Your increased awareness and emotional intelligence have made you better at active reflection: the ability to observe, reflect and make decisions in the moment. Loop's questions will have freed up space in your mind to ask questions as you act. For instance, when career planning you may now ask: is this my definition of success or someone else's? When facing conflict, you may consider whether you are responding as your true self or as your scared self.

Similarly, as you make plans, you will find yourself more able to gauge your commitment to action, and increasingly able to mitigate obstacles. The journal has taken you through the sequence of double loops in such a way that it should start to affect the way you think before you act or make drastic life changes. You will be able to understand your mistakes in new ways, and as you make plans to resolve them, you will check that the original goal reflects your values. This increased integrity and self-knowledge is invaluable. Beyond the journal, you will find yourself double looping naturally.

If you get stuck, you now have the tools to get you moving again; the techniques and questions in Loop can just as easily be used mentally. Next time you have a choice to make, use the system of double looping. Identify what you want the outcome to be, and then challenge yourself to justify it. Check the integrity of your aim to ensure more sustained success. This shouldn't be prolonged rumination. This is rapid and effective introspection. And of course, you can return to Loop at any time.

What you have learned from the content of your journal is of enormous value. Hold on to the process and it will continue to support you. You have started something now: keep going, keep learning and keep looping.

More about the Loop method

The Loop method is based on journaling and underpinned by the idea of Double Loop Learning...

Why journaling?

Journaling is recommended in almost every mental health guide because it works. Studies have demonstrated that journaling in any form helps to improve self-efficacy, the ability to define and make your own choices, and that people who journal have better physical and mental health. They have fewer visits to the doctor, lower blood pressure and improved sleep. These feel like massive claims, but consider the power of a reassuring conversation with a friend; it makes sense that offloading to a neutral page would feel good, even after you have put your pen down. Journaling allows you to activate different areas of the brain, allowing it to create, intuit and feel. Giving yourself ten to fifteen minutes to journal two or three times per week optimizes other parts of the brain. This can allow us to find new answers and develop a deeper understanding of ourselves.

What is Double Loop Learning?

Superficial reflection, which identifies a problem and suggests a solution, is known as Single Loop Learning. For example, if you want to get promoted, the next time your boss asks you to do a presentation, you say yes. What this process doesn't do is examine the previous assumptions and thought patterns that stopped you from saying yes before. If you reflect further, you might realize that you don't really want a promotion at all.

Double Loop Learning, on the other hand, is where real learning and change lies. Identified by Chris Argyris and Donald Schön in their work *Theory in Practice* (1974), Double Loop Learning is a model that was developed for businesses, but which has real value for individuals, too. Every decision you make is built upon layers of past experiences and assumptions. Argyris and Schön call these 'mental maps' and argue that they influence the way we plan, implement and review our actions. They tend to be deeply held and hard to notice.

In a Double Loop, the mental maps that shape our behaviour and decision-making are questioned, empowering us to change or strengthen the way in which we make choices. In Single Loop Learning the goals and frameworks are taken for granted and the emphasis is on making action more effective or efficient. In Double Loop Learning, the motivations and systems themselves are questioned.

You will see the process of Double Looping when you revisit the same page twice and add to your original thoughts, but it is also happening between pages – you don't need to see it for it to be working. All of the activities are designed to express, reflect and capture your ideas. Enjoy them in the moment, then benefit from the cumulative effect. The process will get you out of your comfort zone and into the realm of self-discovery.

It is important to note that the changes that come from Double Loop Learning can be in perspective, feeling and reaction as well as action. Change doesn't have to mean a different situation; it can encompass embracing your current position.

What are the Four Threads in Loop?

The activities in Loop comprise four threads.

Self-awareness: who have I become and why?

This is a chance to really get to know yourself. It is more than tuning into your emotions; it is about developing emotional intelligence. To be emotionally intelligent is to understand that our behaviour, words and actions are shaped by how we feel, and also that they impact those around us. Daniel Goleman's seminal work *Emotional Intelligence: Why it can matter more than IQ* (1996) argues that emotional intelligence counts for twice as much as technical skill and intelligence in determining who will become successful. Having high levels of self-awareness means that we can also perceive how others view us, helping us to observe ourselves honestly; we can see our strengths and limitations, our core values and our wishes. Part of self-awareness is also observing how you came to be, and recognizing how strong voices or experiences have helped form the person you have become. Loop's questions in this category focus on helping you develop a sense of your motivations, core values and ideals, and where they came from.

Next, you have to decide if the person you have become is the person you want to be...

Vision setting: what do I want authentic me to be, feel, think and do?

These activities celebrate your potential and explore possibilities. They are also an essential part of setting accurate goals. One of the reasons that goals aren't achieved is because we didn't spend enough time considering and clarifying our vision. We can identify what we want to do or not do, but these aims are often not integrated into a holistic vision of the life we want. This means that the goals are detached and that we lack motivation when trying to complete them. This journal will help you clarify your vision. It will also help you check that these answers come from your authentic self, and not from fear, pressure or outside influences. Richard Boyatzis called this the discovery of the ideal self in his article from 2006 'The ideal self as the driver of intentional change'. In it, he argues that comparing who you really are with your current persona will provide motivation and a strategy for 'intentional change'. Loop asks you who you want to be, what you want to do and how you want to feel in a number of different ways, encouraging you to consider these questions without limitations, as if money and time were no object. Once you have established your aims, you can reintroduce realism! Spending some time focussing on your vision will make sure that the goals you set are linked to a life you actually want, one that's wholly and authentically yours.

The next step is to consider the tools you already possess to help you progress...

**Need analysis:
what skills and approaches
do I need to enact change?**

During this part of the process, you are encouraged to consider the skills and strengths you have, and might need to develop further, in order to enact change. Part of this is also reflective; you must analyze the ways in which who you have become will both help and hinder this stage of the journey. This involves looking carefully at who you really are, to discover strengths that you can build on and an awareness of any weaknesses. As a result of this process, we are able to make plans and set goals or targets. Some of these may be developmental, some behavioural and others about feelings or thoughts. Some may relate to work or your family and home, others may be spiritual or ethical, social or cultural, mental or educational. Hopefully, the process of looping will ensure that all of the above are linked to your increasingly clear sense of self. You may find that this stage involves looping back to check your assumptions and ideas. Loop encourages you to be bold here: goals that are specific and difficult to achieve will make a greater difference than those that are not. This journal helps develop and grow your self-efficacy, with activities designed to reflect and develop your intrinsic motivation.

Then it is important to look after yourself, to protect and maintain the changes you have made.

**Self-care:
how do I maintain these
changes and care for myself?**

This final thread is about looking after yourself as you enact and maintain changes. It considers how you can assess potential obstacles that may impact your motivation and resilience. It is important for us to acknowledge that relapse, or slippage, is a natural part of any change cycle. What matters more is how we act during and after it. That is why Loop encourages you to revisit your vision and values, to remind yourself of how these new patterns of thought and behaviour fit in, why they matter and why they are worth pursuing. There are things we can do to safeguard ourselves: establishing a community of support, celebrating small wins and caring for others all protect ourselves from our inherent vulnerabilities. Activities in this thread help you to proactively manage threats to your goals or vision, while also ensuring that you care for yourself while on this journey – kindness and support are required at every stage.

Sometimes the process of change making follows a linear structure but more often it does not; you will find that you need to move back and forth between these four strands. For example, to identify your goals, you also have to consider their source and decide whether they are truly yours. When we journal, we journal in our own voice, and the risk is that the book could become an echo chamber. Loop is designed to interrogate long-held ideas to avoid any blind spots. Looping helps to check the integrity of our thoughts and reduces the risk of conformation bias. May it serve you well!

Acknowledgements

This book is the product of much research and many great ideas. I have listed my inspirations here to say thank you, and so that you can take your own adventure further:

Argyris, C.
'Teaching smart people how to learn'
Harvard Business Review, 69 (3): 99–109,
Harvard Business Publishing, 1991.

Argyris, C. & Schon, D.
Theory in Practice
Jossey-Bass, 1974.

Baikie, K. A., Wilhelm, K.
'Emotional and physical health
benefits of expressive writing'
Advances in Psychiatric Treatment, 11:
338–346, Cambridge University Press, 2005.

Boyatzis, R. & Akrivou, K.
'The ideal self as the driver
of intentional change'
Journal of Management Development,
25: 624-642, Emerald Insight, 2006.

Emmons, R. & McCullough, E.
'Counting Blessing Versus Burdens: An
Experimental Investigation of Gratitude
and Subjective Well-Being in Daily Life'
Journal of Personality and Social Psychology,
84 (2): 377–389, 2003.

Fritson, K.
'Impact of Journaling on Students'
Self-Efficacy and Locus of Control'
*InSight: A Journal of Scholarly
Teaching*, 3, 2008.

Gibson, E. & Billings, A.
'Best practices at Best Buy:
a turnaround strategy'
The Journal of Business Strategy,
24(6): 10-16, 2003.

Locke, E.
'Toward a theory of task
motivation and incentives'
*Organizational Behavior and Human
Performance*, 3(2): 157-189, 1968.

Neale, S., Spencer-Arnell, L. & Wilson, L.
Emotional Intelligence Coaching
London: Kogan Page, 2001

Pennebaker, J. W.
'Writing about emotional experiences
as a therapeutic process'
Psychological Science, 8, 162–166, 1997.

Pennebaker, J.W.
*Writing to Heal: A guided journal
for recovering from trauma and
emotional upheaval*
New Harbinger Publications, 2004

Prochaska, J.
Changing for Good
USA: Avon Books, 2000

Purcell, M.
'The Health Benefits of Journaling'
Psych Central 1, 2018

Schön, D.
*The Reflective Practitioner: How
professionals think in action*
USA: Basic Books, 1984

Sinek, S.
Start With Why
London: Penguin, 2011

For my daughter Alice

First published in Great Britain in 2023 by Laurence King,
an imprint of The Orion Publishing Group Ltd
Carmelite House, 50 Victoria Embankment,
London EC4Y 0DZ

An Hachette UK Company

10 9 8 7 6 5 4 3 2 1

A CIP catalogue record for this book is available from the British Library.

ISBN 978-1-3987-0833-4

Design: Therese Vandling

Printed in Malaysia by Vivar Printing Sdn. Bhd.

www.laurenceking.com
www.orionbooks.co.uk